W9-BSI-743

GUIDE TO BARTÓK'S MIKROKOSMOS

Benjamin Suchoff

Revised Edition
(1971)

BOOSEY AND HAWKES
MUSIC PUBLISHERS LIMITED
LONDON
1971

Library of Congress Catalog Card Number

78-138999

Printed in England by

Herbert Fitch & Co. Limited

To My Wife
ELEANOR
this work is gratefully dedicated.

ACKNOWLEDGMENT

The author wishes to express his appreciation to the publishing firm of Boosey and Hawkes, Inc. for permission to reproduce excerpts from the *Mikrokosmos* of Béla Bartók

PREFACE

WHEN Béla Bartók began the composition of the **Mikrokosmos** in 1926, he continued the tradition of important composers writing characteristic and consequential works in the form of teaching pieces (for example, the Bach Inventions). Certain compositions such as the Études of Schumann, Chopin, and Debussy were sparsely annotated by their creators, and this led to the posthumous publication of these works in the form of performing editions and teaching guides which were designed to aid the pianist and piano teacher.

Bartók himself edited works from the standard keyboard repertory; his editions of Bach and Beethoven contain lengthy instructions written in considerable detail.[1] The **Mikrokosmos,** however, is in the category of unedited music although it contains some instructions in its Preface and Notes. In fact, Bartók states in the Preface that "the first three volumes differ from a 'Piano Method' in the traditional sense by the absence of any technical and theoretical description and instruction." Bartók adds that every teacher knows what is required in that respect and is able to give the earliest instruction "without reference to a book or method."

In apparent contradiction to this statement of the composer is the fact that shortly before his death he complied with the request of his publisher (Boosey and Hawkes) to analyze the complete **Mikrokosmos** for a leading piano teacher[2] who was then to disseminate the information by means of lectures to colleagues in the United States. Further, examination of the selected bibliography will disclose the large number of books, theses, and articles devoted to the **Mikrokosmos,** a considerable number of them concerned with pedagogical aspects of the work.

Hence this Guide, written in the form of a manual for pianists and piano teachers. In addition to technical and musical analyses of the entire **Mikrokosmos,** as collated from various sources, are Bartók's comments on his *oeuvre* and my own suggestions on performance and instructional procedures. Preliminary chapters sketch Bartók's career as performer and teacher, present his ideas concerning the way the piano should be played and taught, record and illustrate his objectives in the composition of the **Mikrokosmos,** and relate the work to current educational theory and trends in piano teaching.

---

1 Note also that in collaboration with Alexander Reschofsky he wrote **Zongora Iskola** (Piano School), intended as a manual for teachers of beginning pianists.

2 Ann Chenee, then President of the Piano Teachers Congress of New York.

One of the more important functions of the Index is to serve as a point of reference for the aspiring composer who may be interested in twentieth-century compositional techniques. It should be noted that for practical reasons a complete listing of all the pieces that could serve as examples under each heading or subheading is not given.

It is perhaps worthy of mention here that the Guide represents the combined result of my experience in teaching the **Mikrokosmos** and the findings of my doctoral dissertation **Béla Bartók and a Guide to the Mikrokosmos** (see listing in the Bibliography below).

Some years ago, as a result of a comparison of the various drafts of the **Mikrokosmos** with the published version, my article entitled "Errata in the **Mikrokosmos** Publication" was published in **Piano Quarterly Newsletter** (Summer, 1956). The same information is contained in Volume I of my dissertation. It is to the credit of Boosey and Hawkes, publishers of the **Mikrokosmos,** that the necessary corrections were made in reprinted editions upon exhaustion of original stocks. Owners of the original (1940) edition are advised, therefore, to consult either of the two mentioned sources.

I wish to acknowledge my indebtedness to Ernö Balogh, Ann Chenee, Walter Kob, John Ogden, Halsey Stevens and Susanne Waage. It gives me great pleasure, furthermore, to make special mention of the achievement of my mentor and predecessor–trustee of the Estate of Béla Bartók, the late Victor Bator, who, beginning in 1963, established the New York Bartók Archives. It was my good fortune to serve there as Curator, an experience without which this work might never have reached its present form.

BENJAMIN SUCHOFF

Cedarhurst, New York
July, 1970

CONTENTS

PREFACE v

1. BÉLA BARTÓK 1

2. THE **MIKROKOSMOS** 6

    Rhythm and Polyrhythm 7
    Tonality and Polytonality 8
    Harmonic Principles 9
    Structure 9

3. PEDAGOGY, TECHNIQUE, AND MUSICIANSHIP . 11

    The Relationship of the **Mikrokosmos** to General
      Educational Theory 11
    The **Mikrokosmos** and Trends in Piano Teaching 12
    Bartók's Principles of Piano Teaching 13
    Bartók's Ideas Concerning Piano Playing .. 13
      (a) Percussive Touch-Forms 14
      (b) Non-Percussive Touch-Forms 14
    Bartók's Ideas Concerning Musicianship .. 14
      (a) Dynamics 15
      (b) Rhythm and Tempo 15
      (c) Phrasing 15

4. HOW TO USE THE GUIDE 16

    Format and Definition of Terms 16
    Designations and Abbreviations 18

ANNOTATIONS AND COMMENTARY ON THE
MIKROKOSMOS

    Volume I: Nos. 1-36 (Ex. 1-4) 20
    Volume II: Nos. 37-66 (Ex. 5-18) 36
    Volume III: Nos. 67-96 (Ex. 19-31) 60
    Volume IV: Nos. 97-121 (Ex. 32-33) 86
    Volume V: Nos. 122-139 106
    Volume VI: Nos. 140-153 122

SELECTED BIBLIOGRAPHY 143

INDEX 148

BÉLA BARTÓK

TO commemorate the end of the first fifty years of the twentieth century, the editors of **Etude** magazine canvassed the opinion of musical figures from all parts of the United States to determine the most potent musical forces in this century. The Hungarian composer Béla Bartók was one of the ten musicians selected. Now, only two decades later, Bartók stands astride the twentieth century as its colossus of music, a veritable giant in the three major areas toward which he turned his genius: performance, composition and ethnomusicology.

Devoted son to his widowed mother, husband, father, ardent nationalist, and writer of a voluminous correspondence, Bartók was, in addition, able to pursue a varied musical career. He was active as a concert pianist, composer, student of musical folklore and languages, author of books and articles on music and musicians, and music educator. Any one or two such interests might have been sufficient for a musician of lesser ambition and creative energy. Bartók, however, despite a frail constitution and slowness of acclaim, worked at all with fervor and imagination.

Bartók's career as a pianist began on May 1, 1892, when he appeared at the age of eleven to play his own compositions and a Beethoven sonata in Nagyszőllos, Hungary. As the result of an audition played six years later, Bartók was offered a scholarship at the conservatory in Vienna. This he refused upon the advice of his young mentor, Ernst von Dohnányi, and in 1899 he was admitted to the advanced piano class at the Royal Academy of Music in Budapest, Hungary.

It was during this time, Bartók later related, that he received a special accolade from his teacher, István Thomán, who was considered one of the outstanding piano teachers in Hungary. It seems that when Thomán was a pupil of Liszt, the latter kissed him on the forehead after Thomán had played particularly well. In similar fashion, Thomán kissed the young Bartók, saying, "This kiss is handed down from Liszt!"

After graduation Bartók gave concerts, went on tour as an accompanist, and participated in 1905 in the **Prix Rubinstein** competition as pianist and composer (Wilhelm Backhaus won the piano prize). Due to the apathetic reception accorded to his compositions, Bartók absented himself from public life for a period of eight years beginning in 1912. Then, in 1920, he returned to the concert stage and quickly established a reputation as one of Hungary's ranking pianists. He played Beethoven and Liszt for the most part, few of his own works. His recitals were sell-outs; tickets had to be procured weeks in advance for good seats.

In 1922 Bartók commenced the first of his tours abroad, this time as composer-pianist. Excellent reviews and return engagements attested to his success as a virtuoso. Occasionally he met with mishaps and setbacks in the form of unexpected public reactions. An Italian audience punctuated the close of his Piano Sonata (1926) with a barrage of tomatoes, and several of his performances of the First Piano Concerto were received either in silence punctuated by a few handclaps here and there (Cincinnati, 1928) or by cold applause and boos (Berlin, 1928).

Bartók's self-imposed exile from his native land in 1940 was due to the imminence of a Hungarian alliance with the Axis. He could not remain in a country "so very near to the clutches of the Nazis," and he played his last Hungarian concert in October just prior to sailing for the United States. Gone were his royalties, his pension, and his income from an established concert career. He came to the United States only to find himself still virtually unknown, his works "boycotted" by conductors. He managed to secure a number of concerts and lecture-recitals for the 1940-41 season. These became more and more difficult to obtain and, finally, beset by illness which had plagued him most of his life, and bewildered perhaps by the unfriendly reviews of provincial critics, he played his last public concert on January 21, 1943, at Carnegie Hall in New York City.

It has been in comparatively recent years, and after his death, that Bartók has been equated as a pianist with Walter Gieseking and Alexander Borowsky, or referred to as a piano virtuoso who could have become one of the world's foremost pianists had he not chosen to devote the major portion of his time and energy to composition and ethnomusicology.

To most persons the name Bartók brings to mind a picture of the man as composer. In fact, it has been remarked that not since Mozart has a composer come so quickly into general recognition solely as the result of the interest in his music stirred up by the accident of his death in 1945.

He composed or transcribed more than 100 works for the various musical media and, within ten years after his death, few of them remained which had not been published or recorded. Outstanding are the six string quartets, the three concertos for piano and the two for violin, the opera **Duke Bluebeard's Castle,** the ballets **Miraculous Mandarin** and **Wooden Prince,** the **Concerto for Orchestra, Cantata Profana, For Children,** and **Mikrokosmos.** The last-named work is considered by a number of sources to be Bartók's musical testament.

His music is rooted in East European peasant music, particularly that of Bulgaria, Hungary, Rumania, Slovakia and Yugoslavia. The principle underlying his style of composition is the assimilation of the idiom of peasant music to the extent that its use becomes subconscious, a musical mother-tongue. To do so, Bartók has said, one must have lived by direct contact with the peasants in their own environment. His objective as a composer was the fusion of East and West; that is, fusion of folk melody and rhythm with pre-classic contrapuntal treatment, classic progressive form, and the harmonic possibilities of Impressionism. The integrating element: modality.[1] The aim: to avoid the "excesses" of romanticism and, at the same time, to emphasize the expressive ability of tonal music (contrary to the opinion and practice of twelve-tone composers, the so-called "atonalists").

While a student at the Academy, Bartók began the composition of **Kossuth,** a symphonic poem depicting the events in Louis Kossuth's struggle against the Hapsburg Monarchy. Bordering on the Lisztian concept of Hungarian music: gypsy music, **Kossuth** led to a dead end in Bartók's search for a new way to create something specifically Hungarian. He suspected that the gypsy music which was then considered as the true Hungarian music was in reality an urbanization of music of peasant origin. His study of Zoltán Kodály's 1905 publication of Hungarian folk songs confirmed that suspicion and prompted the first of his many field trips to record the peasant music of Hungarian and neighboring peoples.

Bartók's researches in ethnomusicology were important enough to gain for him a position as a member of the Hungarian Academy of Science in 1936. Here he began work on the vast amount of material

---

1 But a peculiarly Bartókian modality. Space here does not permit other than the brief mention of Bartók's use of modes bitonally, in alternation, transposed, and as compound structures in which "color" tones are borrowed from several modes built on the same principal tone. A more detailed discussion appears in the next chapter.

collected in the past. Not long after he arrived in the United States he received a grant from Columbia University to investigate the Parry collection of recorded Yugoslav folk music. The work of forty years of research is summarized in five large volumes on Rumanian folk music, and in one or more equally lengthy studies on Hungarian, Serbo-Croatian, Slovak, and Turkish folk music, less than half of them published during his lifetime[2], and a considerable number of smaller publications and magazine articles. All led to his being known and acclaimed internationally as an outstanding comparative music-ologist.[3]

From time to time Bartók wrote articles on composers such as Liszt, Schoenberg, Kodály, and Richard Strauss, and on contemp-orary music—Hungarian art music in particular. He was also a contributor to general and music reference books.

As an aid to his folk music studies, since he was involved with the morphology of the language he happened to be working with, Bartók compiled his own dictionaries constructed of foolscap which were folded and crudely bound with cord in the form of notebooks. His interest in linguistics extended to the practice of drawing Arabic and Chinese characters, and to the writing of polyglot letters to his correspondents. Bartók's basic language was, of course, Hungarian, and he had an almost equal command of German and French. Lecture notes, documents, and unpublished books reveal his mastery of the English language which he spoke hesitatingly and with a rather heavy accent. He also read and wrote Rumanian with similar ease, but could not speak the language with any degree of fluency. For his own purposes, he had an adequate knowledge of Slavic tongues and a nodding acquaintanceship with Arabic and Turkish. To these should be added the Spanish language which he took up in 1906 when he accompanied the violin prodigy Ferenc Vecsey to the Iberian peninsula.

First experiences as a music educator occurred prior to the turn of the century when Bartók began teaching the piano privately. As many another neophyte, he soon discovered the financial problems involved in such employment, especially when he needed to augment the funds received from his mother (his father died when Bartók was eight years old) for food and lodging during his student years.

---

2 Vols. I-III of **Rumanian Folk Music** were published in 1967, Vols. IV-V in 1971 by Martinus Nijhoff (The Hague) and were edited by the present writer.

3 It is perhaps not generally known that Bartók considered his folk music research of more significance than his composition. Much of his concertising was done to secure funds needed to finance his research work and to pay for the publication of certain folk music collections.

He was but twenty-six years of age when he was appointed Professor of Piano at the Academy to succeed his teacher (Thomán) upon the latter's retirement. Here Bartók taught the advanced piano class, and he taught the piano privately in his own home up to the year of his death.

Following his Academy appointment, he edited piano music in the standard keyboard repertory. The list of such editions is impressive: Bach's **Well-Tempered Keyboard**[4], Beethoven, Haydn, Mozart, and Scarlatti Sonatas, pieces by Couperin, Purcell, and other Baroque composers, Mendelssohn and Schubert Scherzi, and the Schumann **Album for the Young.** Bartók's efforts were also directed towards the music education of children, and in 1913 he and Alexander Reschofsky collaborated in the writing of a Piano School (**Zongora Iskola**), a method for the teaching of beginners, still in use in Hungary and published in German and Scandinavian editions in 1953, and in English in 1968. The **Mikrokosmos** itself was compiled in the form of a piano method as a result of Bartók's experiences in teaching his son, Peter, the piano.

The composer was honored repeatedly during his career. Outstanding among his awards were Chevalier of the Legion of Honor (France, 1930), the honorary degree of Doctor of Music (Columbia University, 1940), and Member of the New Hungarian Parliament (elected *in absentia* by the people of Budapest, 1945). In Hungary after his death, streets, roads, squares and a music conservatory were named after him, commemorative stamps bearing his likeness were issued, a plaque was placed on the doorway of his former residence, and a motion picture about him released in 1955. In other countries Bartók societies were organized, music festivals held and special magazine issues published. A Bartók archive was established in New York and in Budapest to collect and preserve all matter written by and about the composer. Today, libraries everywhere contain books devoted in whole or in part to the composer's life and music, and television films and programs on Bartók are frequently scheduled in America and Europe.

It has been said that Béla Bartók may well be one of those found to form a major part of the music of the future. In the **Mikrokosmos,** in a most accessible form for amateur and professional musicians alike, are the keys to Bartók's world of music.

---

4 Bartók's own title for "The 48 Preludes and Fugues" which he proposed as the most appropriate translation of Bach's **Wohltemperiertes Klavier.**

THE MIKROKOSMOS

SHORTLY after Bartók's career as a concert pianist became established on an international scale in the 1920's, his need for recital pieces seems to have provided him with the impetus to compose piano works. The **Improvisations, Op.** 20, had been written in 1920, and five more years were to elapse before he was to resume composing for the keyboard. Then, in a burst of creative energy, he wrote the **Piano Sonata,** the **First Piano Concerto, Out of Doors,** and **Nine Little Piano Pieces.** The last-named work was assembled from a collection of more than twelve compositions; three of them eventually became part of the **Mikrokosmos.**[1]

Bartók's initial concept of the **Mikrokosmos,** therefore, was of the work as a collection of recital pieces, and he gave the first performance of seventeen of them in London on February 9, 1937.

The year before, Bartók began teaching his son Peter the piano, and he wrote little pieces and exercises for the boy. In characteristic fashion the composer became absorbed in the problems involved in the early grades of piano playing. He decided to arrange the **Mikrokosmos** as a collection of pieces in progressive order of technical and musical difficulty, he consulted with at least one Hungarian authority on piano pedagogy, and he used his son as a "guinea pig" until such time as the pieces were composed faster than Peter could learn them (the first two volumes are dedicated to "Péteré"). Then the father composed the **Mikrokosmos** independent of any consideration of its suitability for the son, completing the work in November, 1939.

The **Mikrokosmos** may also be interpreted as a series of pieces in different styles. One can find idioms representative of composers such as Couperin (no. 117), Bach (nos. 79 and 91), Schumann (no. 80), and Gershwin (no. 151. See Index for other listings). Highly chromatic examples have been quoted as compromise solutions from the perspective of the twelve-tone composition principle (nos. 91, 100, 132, and 147). Abstract music (nos. 45 and 81) and program pieces (to mention a few: nos. 15, 72, and 130) are further examples of the eclecticism of the work.

---

1 **Unisono** (no. 137), **Wandering** (no. 81), and **Ostinato** (no. 146). Of the three, **Unisono** was the first completed and, therefore, it may be considered to be the first piece composed for the **Mikrokosmos.**

In his lecture-recitals, Bartók said that a purpose of the **Mikrokosmos** is to provide an opportunity for pianists to become acquainted with the simple and non-romantic beauties of folk music. The collection serves also as an admirable illustration of the ways in which its composer transmutes peasant into art music. One type is that in which accompaniment, introductory and concluding phrases are of secondary importance to the peasant melody (nos. 74 and 127). In another, the melody only serves as a motto while that which is built round it is of real importance (nos. 100, 112, and 115). A third method is one in which a real peasant melody is not used but rather an imitation of it is invented (nos. 90 and 128). A fourth kind of transmutation does not contain peasant melodies or their imitation but is pervaded by the atmosphere of peasant music (no. 111).

Apparently another aim of the **Mikrokosmos** is to teach students the elements of music composition by means of contemporary procedures.[2] In fact, a considerable number of sources refer to the work as a textbook for composers.

RHYTHM AND POLYRHYTHM

Syncopation patterns occur in more than forty per cent of the pieces comprising the **Mikrokosmos;** indeed, one source has determined the existence of 636 different syncopation patterns, some of them recurring in several pieces.

Beginning with the first volume (no. 12), metrical changes in one piece are not infrequently encountered. No. 140 seems to be a study in that respect for it contains thirty-seven changes of time.

Additive or irregular rhythms appear in the second volume (no. 48:5/4) and increase in complexity in later volumes, such as No. 152: $2+2+2+3$.

8

The conflicting coincidence of different rhythms, also referred to as cross-rhythm or polyrhythm, can be found in nos. 97, 130, and 138. A more intricate polyrhythm is one in which non-coinciding meters are employed (no. 138: although the measure signature is 2/4 the left hand plays syncopated melodic intervals which give the effect of a drone bass in triple meter and, at the same time, the right hand plays a melody whose rhythmic emphasis is strongly duple). Other examples of non-coinciding or overlapping meters occur in nos. 103, 110, 124-5, 129, 131, 133, 145, and 146.

2 This objective has not been attributed to the composer.

TONALITY AND POLYTONALITY

The **Mikrokosmos** pieces are based on various scale systems, the majority of them pentatonic (for example, no. 61) or modal (nos. 32, 34, 36-7, and 48, among others). Other examples: major-minor system (no. 103), chromatic (no. 54), Oriental or Arabic type with a minor third and an augmented fourth (no. 58), whole-tone (no. 136), and artificial or Bartók-devised scales such as

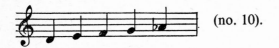 (no. 10).

Bartók employs three types of melodic patterns with reference to modal construction. The first type of melody is in an ecclesiastic mode (no. 31: Dorian) which may retain its "purity" also in transposed form (no. 24: *D* Lydian). In the second case, the melody alternates between different modes (no. 53: major and Dorian). The third type of melody is in a specific tonality but with one or more altered notes—called "color" or "foreign" tones by Bartók—borrowed from other modes built on the same principal tone (no. 92: Phrygian mode with augmented or Lydian fourth).

Harmonic procedure in the **Mikrokosmos** can serve as a basis for understanding the manner in which Bartók applies the concept of polytonality, the simultaneous use of different tonalities. The first and simplest stage is the interaction of two pure modes which have identical principal tones (no. 59: upper voice in *F* minor, lower voice in *F* Lydian, interchanging at measures 7-12 and again at measures 13-18). Second, two modes may interact—each with a different principal tone—so that one is stronger than the other (no. 122: upper voice in *G* major, lower voice in *C* Lydian). Third, the different principal tones may be of equal intensity so that a kind of "neutral tonality" takes place (no. 101: upper voice is Aeolian, lower voice is *E♭* Dorian). Fourth, the interaction of compound modes which have the same principal tone (no. 117: measures 1-4 are essentially *D* Mixolydian, with Phrygian color in the upper and the Lydian fourth in the lower voice. Measures 17-21 are comprised of a pure Mixolydian mode transposed to *D* in the upper and *D* Lydian with Aeolian color in the lower voice). What may be the highest stage in terms of complexity is the interaction of two compounded tonal systems, each with a different principal tone (no. 121: measures 1-3 are in *E* Mixolydian with Lydian color in the upper and *D* Lydian with Aeolian color in the lower voice).

HARMONIC PRINCIPLES

Bartók writes that his use of the chord of the seventh as a concord was prompted by his folk music researches in which the seventh appears as an interval of equal importance with the third and fifth. Examples of such usage can be found in the **Mikrokosmos** (nos. 78 and 105: final chord).

He states further that the frequent use of quart intervals suggested the use of quart chords. Quartal harmony (chords built of successive fourths, rather than of thirds as in the tertian system) in the **Mikrokosmos** exists in arpeggio form (no. 125) and as chords (**ossia**, no. 131).

Nos. 132 and 144 contain tone clusters in arpeggio form. In chord form: nos. 107, 130, 132, and 142.

The discovery of "a highly interesting treatment of the Tritone" in Rumanian and Slovakian folk songs led Bartók to the free use of the augmented fourth and diminished fifth (in the **Mikrokosmos**: no. 101).

STRUCTURE

Certain of the pieces comprising Volume I of the method contain what Bartók terms irregular or asymmetrical phrases. For example, four groups of three-measure phrases (no. 3), five phrases which are two or three measures in length (no. 5), three phrases of four, three, and two measure lengths (no. 6), and so forth.

Among the various cadence formulas in the work are those in which a major chord ends a piece in the minor mode (no. 32) and in which an ending frequently used in Yugoslav music occurs (no. 26: the closing chord is on the dominant with the fifth in the bass and the second degree in the soprano voice). Other Bartókian devices: closing on a tonic six-four chord (no. 87), on the interval of the diminished fifth (no. 101), and on the simultaneous sounding of the leading tone against the tonic, the latter then tied over into the last measure as its only tone (no. 121). No. 73 contains a plagal and no. 128 a Phrygian cadence.

Just about every device of the contrapuntist can be located in the **Mikrokosmos:** imitation (no. 22 ff.) and stretto-like writing (no. 58), inversion of voices (no. 23 ff.) and intervals (no. 29 ff.), strict and free canon (nos. 31 and 36 respectively), augmentation and diminution (no. 46), retrograde motion (nos. 92 and 96), and pedal or organ point (no. 128).

Melodic construction consists either of long lines with half and authentic cadences (no. 68) or, for the most part, short, iterative motives (for example, the upper part of no. 69).

Bartók has defined the **ostinato** as a ground bass which recurs obstinately throughout a composition, and he has said that its traditional use was in the form of a repeated theme (nos. 47 and 148) rather than repeated chords (no. 146) or intervals (no. 138: perfect fifths as a drone bass).

Structural schemata of Hungarian music, Bartók discovered, can be placed in two general classifications: architectonic, or rounded in form, and non-architectonic, or non-rounded. The former is the familiar AABA form (as in nos. 12 and 13) and the latter is comprised of ABBC (no. 106), AABB (nos. 14 and 53), AABC (nos. 7, 28 and 79), ABAB (nos. 42 and 51), and ABCD (nos. 9 and 86). Other symmetrical structures to be found in the **Mikrokosmos** but not in the peasant music of Hungary are ABA and ABCA, other non-rounded forms include AB, ABC, ABCDE, and ABCDC.

Fourteen pieces are in free form, such as nos. 102 and 151, the result of Bartók's improvisatory treatment of fragmentary musical ideas.

Major forms include the theme and variations (nos. 45, 72, and 148), the rondo (nos. 107, 150 and 152) and what might be termed a "rondo-variation" form (nos. 57, 128, 136, and 141), since the thematic repetitions are varied to some extent.

CHAPTER 3

PEDAGOGY, TECHNIQUE, AND MUSICIANSHIP

IT has been stated by several sources that no music is liable to lose so much as Béla Bartók's at the hands of executants; indeed, that the performer, no matter how technically skilled, must be in sympathy with and have an insight into Bartók's intentions.

But what were Bartók's intentions, particularly with reference to his piano works? Fortunately the composer left documents which provide data capable of assembly into specifics of pedagogy, technique, and musicianship that may be useful as an approach to Bartók's piano works in general and the **Mikrokosmos** in particular. There are the composer's illustrated lecture notes on piano playing and other unpublished materials, his edited piano works from the standard repertory, the **Mikrokosmos** Preface and Notes, and the Bartók-Reschofsky elementary piano method. Further, we have the evidence of his own piano recordings and of his former piano pupils. All indicate that he was aware of educational theory and trends in piano teaching, that he followed certain principles in his role as music educator, and that he had definite ideas concerning the way the piano should be played.

THE RELATIONSHIP OF THE MIKROKOSMOS TO GENERAL EDUCATIONAL THEORY. Bartók was quite aware of individual differences among piano pupils. For example, in the Preface to the **Mikrokosmos** he refers to "gifted" and "less gifted" pupils. In his unpublished notes he refers also to such learners as "average" and "unusual" pupils. It seems likely that Bartók's interpretation of these designations is in terms of co-ordination, for in the latter source he refers also to "the pupil who has great control." Too, Bartók recommends the following procedures to meet individual needs: (a) the order of pieces may be altered in accordance with the ability of the pupil, (b) many of the pieces may be played faster or slower than indicated, (c) teacher and pupil have the opportunity of making a choice, since there are frequently several pieces dealing with the same problem, (d) the teacher should invent exercises for the pupil, and (e) the teacher should "present pieces in any way that seems best to the student's needs."

An indication of the composer's desire to stimulate pupil interest in the **Mikrokosmos** can be seen in the number of pieces which contain attractive titles, such as: **Boating, Dragons' Dance, Wrestling, From the Island of Bali,** and so forth. Bartók believed that certain pieces were interesting because of their construction in terms of unusual rhythmic patterns, changes of meter or tempo, hand crossings, colorful tonality, use of the pedal, or irregularity of phrase structure.

The satisfaction that comes with success is of the greatest importance in arousing readiness toward piano playing. The first three volumes of the **Mikrokosmos** seem to have been compiled with that thought in mind, for they are comprised of short pieces (many of them sixteen measures in length, or less), written within a five-finger range, which are arranged in graded order according to difficulty. And there are equally brief preparatory exercises to a third of the pieces.

THE MIKROKOSMOS AND TRENDS IN PIANO TEACHING. In the Preface to **Mikrokosmos,** Bartók asserts that "Instrumental tuition should be developed from suitable singing exercises." This, one of the fundamental concepts of Jaques-Dalcroze and of public school music education, is developed in the method through the inclusion of pieces for voice and piano to be sung and self-accompanied by the pupil.

One of the important elements in piano playing is the ability to play as freely in one key as in another. In accordance with this principle, Bartók recommends the transposition of the easier pieces and exercises into other keys. It will be noted also that the pieces in the **Mikrokosmos** are written in a variety of keys and, furthermore, they are not limited to the Western major-minor tonal system.

Bartók also understood the value of creative expression as a means of stimulating pupil interest and of encouraging good practice habits. He suggests that the pupil should transcribe suitable pieces (from the first three volumes of the **Mikrokosmos**) for two pianos, and he states that many opportunities are given for original and inventive work in terms of simplification of accompaniments and "other developments."

Finally, the **Mikrokosmos** exemplifies the philosophy of theory through practice. The fundamentals of musicianship are introduced one by one in the interesting materials at hand to such an extent that the use of the **Mikrokosmos** as part of the lesson plan can be said to obviate the necessity of piano teachers conducting separate theory classes for their pupils.

BARTÓK'S PRINCIPLES OF PIANO TEACHING

Throughout his teaching career Béla Bartók believed that musicianship preceded and formed the foundation for performance at the piano. In fact, he said that "One cannot be a pianist without being a musician." It should not be inferred that Bartók was not concerned with technical development; indeed, in the Preface to **Mikrokosmos** he suggests "the appropriate studies by Czerny, etc." But he assigned greater value to musicianship, for he conceived of technique as the means rather than the end in piano playing.

A second fundamental principle was the extension of his philosophy of performance to his teaching; to follow the intention of the composer as expressed in the written score. His attention was directed also to the smallest of details, and he did not permit deviations unless they could be justified by the pupil.

Demonstrational teaching was an important part of Bartók's piano lessons, and he would replay again and again at the piano to illustrate a particular point. Apparently Bartók was a patient man who was endowed with seeming tirelessness when it came to demonstrating for his pupils.

BARTÓK'S IDEAS CONCERNING PIANO PLAYING

Bartók's conception of the piano was in terms of its being an instrument capable of producing sounds ranging from the most to the least percussive in quality, and he specified key-striking, the so-called "percussive touch" as the basic way the piano is to be played. In fact, it is only in terms of percussive finger-stroke as the fundamental approach to key depression that the symbols Bartók uses in the **Mikrokosmos** take on their full meaning. For example, pianists usually interpret the **tenuto** sign as a dynamic accent of weak intensity or as an indication that a note is to be held for its full value. Bartók, however, adds a third meaning: "To such notes a certain color shading must be added by pressing the key instead of striking it."

The touch-forms used in the **Mikrokomos** are listed below together with their descriptions as set down by Bartók in his other pedagogical works and editions for the piano.

(a) PERCUSSIVE TOUCH-FORMS.

Staccatissimo ❜ ❜ ❜ is an increased **staccato** in which the tone becomes the shortest possible.

Staccato • • • means that the sounding of the note ranges from the shortest in value to one-half the value of the note.

Non-legato is played (when no other touch-form designations appear in the music) so that the gap between two tones is imperceptibly small.

Legato is indicated by the use of curved lines or the sign **legato.**

Legatissimo is an exaggerated **legato:** when every tone is held over a little into the beginning of the next one. It can be perfected by using the half-pedal. It is used when the music is marked **legatissimo.**

(b) NON-PERCUSSIVE TOUCH-FORMS.

Tenuto − − − is a kind of warning that the note is more important and colorful and therefore should be maintained in its full value. To such notes a certain color shading must be added by pressing the key instead of striking it. It is played with weight.

Dotted **Tenuto** ⁔⁔⁔ means that the notes are never less than one-half their value and that they are to be played with the **tenuto** touch. Also played with weight.

Portamento ⁔ • • is in close connection with dotted **tenuto.** They have one difference: it is necessary to play **portamento** lightly (without weight).

Espressivo (with expression) and **dolce** (with softness) cannot be learned by description. The student can acquire them only if the teacher demonstrates at the piano. The so-called **espressivo** touch is played with hand-motion.

(The playing of **marcato** > and **sforzato** _sf_ should be carried out by the fingers and should not be perceivable in the hand. In this touch the position of the fingers does not change).

BARTÓK'S IDEAS CONCERNING MUSICIANSHIP

The composer was careful to indicate in the **Mikrokosmos** exactly how he wanted the work played. In fact, almost all the pieces contain three tempo indications (tempo marks, metronome marks, and time of performance); dynamic markings; explanatory terms; and other symbols to the extent that the work can be considered to be not unlike a dictionary of music.

In the discussion of Bartók's teaching principles (above), it is pointed out that he emphasized truth in interpretation. In accordance with this philosophy, listed below are a number of signs whose meaning may be obscure or open to more than one interpretation, together with Bartók's specific instructions as assembled from his other pedagogical works and editions for the piano.

(a) **DYNAMICS**

sff, *sf* (**sforzato**), ∧ (**marcatissimo**) and > (**marcato**) are dynamic accents listed in order of diminishing emphasis.[1]

A dynamic sign is effective until replaced by another.

A **decrescendo** takes place towards the second of two slurred notes.

Accents within the frame of *p* are weaker than within the frame of *f*.

Syncopated notes should be played with some weight and emphasis.

(b) **RHYTHM AND TEMPO.**

The first part of each measure receives the chief emphasis.

Sostenuto indicates a sudden **ritardando.**

The fermata ⌒ about doubles the value of the note beneath it.

(c) **PHRASING.**

Curved lines are used to indicate **legato,** and they also mark the phrasing. **Legato** phrases are not to be separated where the curved lines meet unless they are marked with separating signs. **Legato** phrases can be emphasized, however, by beginning them with a slight dynamic shading.

When two slurs meet at one note, the phrase begins and ends at that note.

The **separating sign** | indicates the interruption of **legato** between phrases. The last note of the phrase preceding this sign should be played **staccato** or otherwise shortened.

The separating sign ' (**comma**) also indicates the interruption of **legato.** In this case, it means a slight, almost unnoticeable pause in which the time of separation is taken equally from the notes preceding and following the comma.

---

1 **Tenuto,** the weakest of accents, is not listed here in order to emphasize its primary function as a (non-percussive) touch-form. See preceding page.

HOW TO USE THE 'GUIDE'

FORMAT AND DEFINITION OF TERMS.

OF the four major headings used in the description of the pieces, A. **Technique** and B. **Musicianship** represent the findings of the author and other analysts of the **Mikrokosmos;** C. **Bartók's Comments** contains extracts from the Preface and Notes to **Mikrokosmos** and, what is perhaps more important, Béla Bartók's unpublished notes on the pedagogy of the **Mikrokosmos** (given to Ann Chenee in July, 1944); and D. **Suggestions** includes the experiences of the author and other teachers of the **Mikrokosmos,** and references to certain recordings of the **Mikrokosmos** and its transcriptions for two pianos (four hands), **Seven Pieces from "Mikrokosmos"** (published by Boosey and Hawkes).

For the purposes of clarity and conciseness, the categories concerned with technique and musicianship are divided further into appropriate first-order and second-order subheads. These, together with an explanation of their use, are as follows:

A. **Technique.**
   1. TOUCH: the various **legato** touch-forms (**legato, legatissimo, espressivo, dolce,** and **cantabile**) and **non-legato** touch-forms (**non-legato, tenuto,** dotted **tenuto, portamento** or **portato, staccato,** and **staccatissimo**).

   2. HAND INDEPENDENCE: the dissociate movement or separate function of the hands. It includes:
      (a) Counterpoint: the simultaneous playing, between the hands, of two or more independent parts.
      (b) Combined Touch-Forms: **legato** in one hand as the other hand plays **staccato,** etc.
      (c) Dynamic Contrast: the playing of **marcato** in one hand as the other hand maintains a consistent dynamic level, etc.

(d) Accompanying Figurations: the playing of **ostinato**-like patterns (motives, intervals, chords, or broken chords) in one hand as the other hand plays a melody which may or may not require dynamic contrast.

3. FINGER INDEPENDENCE: the simultaneous playing, in one hand, of two independent parts. In the **Mikrokosmos** this consists for the most part of sustained tones against a moving voice.

4. INTERVAL, CHORD, AND/OR BROKEN CHORD PLAYING: The **Mikrokosmos** contains harmonic intervals up to and including a tenth; triads and their inversions, various types of chords comprised of three or more tones; and arpeggios, of which none involve passing of the thumb.

5. POSITION: five-finger range; two or more changes of position; the hands one or more octaves apart; interlocking of the hands; and crossing of the hands in which the right or the left hand crosses over (**sopra**) or under (**sotto**).

6. PEDALLING: Use of the damper or solo **sostenuto** pedals as indicated in the **Mikrokosmos.** There is no specific indication in the work for use of the soft pedal.

7. PASSAGE-WORK: scalar-type passages, usually in quick tempo, which may or may not involve passing of the fingers.

8. EMBELLISHMENTS: grace notes, turns, the **pralltriller** (inverted mordent), fast or slow trills, and fast or slow tremolos (trills comprised of intervals greater than a second).

9. FINGERING PROBLEMS: black key playing (particularly with the first and fifth fingers), "discontinuous" fingerings, replacement of fingers, and so forth.

10. ENSEMBLE PLAYING. Vocal or instrumental accompanying and the performance of pieces for two pianos (four hands).

B. **Musicianship.**

1. NOTATION: note and rest values, clef changes, key signatures, accidentals, pitch names, and various characters used in music notation.

2. RHYTHM: meter signatures, change of time, non-coinciding or overlapping meters, sub-division of the beat, cross-rhythm (polyrhythm), and syncopation.

3. EXPRESSION: the fundamentals of musicianship concerned with

   (a) Tempo: metronome marks; tempo changes; and various signs indicating steady, accelerating, or slackening rate of speed.

   (b) Dynamics: accents; symbols (*pp* to *fff*); and various signs which maintain or change levels of intensity.

   (c) Phrasing: regularity or irregularity of phrase structure, certain cadences, and aspects of form (ternary, rondo, and theme and variations).

   (d) Terms: other directions (for example, **la seconda volta**), and character signs with more than one expressive meaning (**stringendo**).

All descriptions and instructions are given in outline form, and it is expected that the teacher will refer to the published volumes of the **Mikrokosmos** when using the GUIDE.

DESIGNATIONS AND ABBREVIATIONS

Keys or tonality centers are indicated in the GUIDE by italicized capitals, and specific pitches are identified by italicized lower-case letters. A word (or words) in double quotation marks refers to a direction or statement made by Béla Bartók in his other pedagogical works for the piano.

In D. **Suggestions,** reference also is made to Béla Bartók's recording of the **Mikrokosmos** (Columbia ML 4419). In order to help the pianist locate quickly a particular piece in this long-playing record, the following type of instruction is given: "See BR 1:6:2". The first numeral designates the side of the record, the second indicates the number of the band, and the third refers to the order of the piece within that band (there are as many as four pieces recorded in one band).[1] Béla and Ditta Bartók's recording of certain transcriptions from the **Mikrokosmos** are referred to with the instructions "See REMINGTON R19994."[2]

Other abbreviations:

against (versus)	—	*vs.*
beat(s)	—	*b. (B.)*
left hand	—	*L.H.*
right hand	—	*R.H.*
measure(s)	—	*m. (M.)*
Exercise	—	*Ex.*

1 Side 1 appears in exact duplication on the first side of **Bartók: Mikrokosmos/Contrasts,** Odyssey (Columbia) 32-16-0220 (Library of Congress No. R68-2564).

2 Also published as Continental 4008. The Bartók recordings are, for the most part, restricted to the last three volumes of the **Mikrokosmos.** The attention of the reader, therefore, is directed to the complete recording of the Mikrokosmos as played by Bartók's greatest pupil, György Sandor (Columbia SL-229, also Vox VBX-425). Of equal importance, of course, is Ditta Pásztory Bartók's (Mrs. Béla Bartók) recording of selections from each of the six volumes of the **Mikrokosmos.** (Mace (Qualiton, Budapest) M-9007. See also Qualiton 1110, 1033-35). Older recordings are listed in **A Memorial Review** (Boosey & Hawkes, 1950), p.80.

ANNOTATIONS AND COMMENTARY
ON THE MIKROKOSMOS

VOLUME I
Nos. 1-36
(Ex. 1-4)

Nos. 1-6. Six Unison Melodies.
  A. **Technique.**
     1. TOUCH. **Legato.**
     2. POSITION. One, the hands an octave or two octaves apart.
  B. **Musicianship.**
     1. NOTATION. Whole, half, and quarter notes. Half and quarter rests. The phrase mark.
     2. RHYTHM. 4/4.
     3. EXPRESSION.
        (a) Phrasing: regular and irregular structure.

  C. **Bartók's Comments.** Melodies are scalewise with consistent note values and five-finger range. Small staves above each piece indicate range of five-finger position. Nos. 1 and 2 are symmetrical or balanced in phrase structure. No. 3 is written in a sort of *D* minor beginning on the dominant. No. 4 contains combinations of note values in shorter sentences, and it begins on the seventh tone and ends in *C*. No. 5 is in the natural *A* minor; it contains a stepwise sequence of asymmetrical phrases. No. 6 begins and ends on the fifth tone, and it introduces the quarter rest.

  D. **Suggestions.** The melodies written two octaves apart should foster good elbow position (check this during the playing of no. 3). In m. 6 of no. 6, do not give the half note less than its full value in anticipation of the quarter rest.

Try several transpositions according to Bartók's recommendation in the Preface to **Mikrokosmos.**

No. 7. Dotted Notes.

 A. **Technique.**
   1. TOUCH. **Legato.**

 B. **Musicianship.**
   1. NOTATION. The dotted half note.

 C. **Bartók's Comments.** This melody is also used in no. 28. Dotted notes in the Phrygian Mode. The rhythm can be illustrated in this way:

 D. **Suggestions.** It is perhaps in order here to call attention to the composer's instruction that no interruption of **legato** should take place between **legato** phrases.

No. 8. Repetition.

 A. **Technique.**
   1. TOUCH. **Legato, non-legato.**
   2. FINGERING PROBLEMS. Black key playing.
   3. POSITION. Five-note range in two positions.

 B. **Musicianship.**
   1. NOTATION. Key of *G*.

 C. **Bartók's Comments.** In the key signature it is more convenient to put the sharp on the same space as the note. It is easier to see, too. Combination of rests. Theme is inverted. Short phrases because of repeated notes.

 D. **Suggestions.** First example of change of hand position. A Bartók-devised key signature which the composer used in his folk music notation. The sharp sign usually appears on the fifth line of the treble clef. The gap between the repeated notes should be "hardly perceivable."

No. 9. Syncopation.

 A. **Technique.**
   1. TOUCH. **Legato.**

B. **Musicianship.**
  1. NOTATION. The tie.
  2. RHYTHM. Syncopation.

C. **Bartók's Comments.** The rhythmic feeling of the suspensions should be emphasized by some energetic movement, such as tapping with the foot, nodding the head, or using the voice in the respective places which are marked by rhythm signatures between the staves. This melody is also used in no. 27.

D. **Suggestions.** Be sure that the half note is given its full value in m. 12, and note that the phrase markings in M. 8-14 indicate that the third phrase ends and the last phrase begins on the same tone (*g*).

No. 10.   With Alternate Hands.

A. **Technique.**
  1. TOUCH. **Legato.**
  2. FINGERING PROBLEMS. Black key playing.

B. **Musicianship.**
  1. NOTATION. Bartók-devised key signature.
  2. RHYTHM. 3/4 Syncopation.

C. **Bartók's Comments.** The signature is *A♭*. Lowered fifth for special color. Combines past experiences.

D. **Suggestions.** Accent slightly the half notes in

M. 18   and 21.

No. 11.   Parallel Motion.

A. **Technique.**
  1. TOUCH. **Legato.**

B. **Musicianship.**
  1. NOTATION. Reading of two voices which proceed in similar motion at the interval of a tenth.

C. **Bartók's Comments.** Mixolydian, beginning on the second degree. Voices proceed at the interval of a tenth.

D. **Suggestions.** Do not overlook the contrary motion between M. 14 and 15. Take notice of the metronome mark.

No. 12.   Reflection.

   A. **Technique.**

      1. TOUCH. **Legato.**

      2. HAND INDEPENDENCE.

         (a) Counterpoint.

   B. **Musicianship.**

      1. RHYTHM. Change of time: 2/2 and 3/2. Subdivision of the beat into two parts, the half note as the pulse unit.

C. **Bartók's Comments.** Present the time signatures in any way that seems best to the student's needs. Bitonal—contrast of major (L.H.) and minor (R.H.) modes. The left hand reflects the right hand, and the voices move in opposite direction. The structure is more lively due to change of meter.

D. **Suggestions.** The voices move in *parallel* motion between

M. 16 and 17.

No. 13.   Change of Position.

   A. **Technique.**

      1. TOUCH. **Legato.**

      2. POSITION. Five-note range in two positions.

   B. **Musicianship.**

      1. EXPRESSION.

         (a) Phrasing: symmetrical phrases in ternary form.

C. **Bartók's Comments.** The same melody is used in no. 17.

D. **Suggestions.** The first and last phrases are identical, and the second is similar (five tones higher) to the first phrase. Mark the phrases A A⁵ B A. Such analysis is valuable in determining identical portions of a composition, thus making for its quicker mastery or easier memorization.

No. 14.   Question and Answer.

A. **Technique.**

    1. TOUCH. **Legato.**

    2. POSITION. Five-note range in three positions.

    3. ENSEMBLE PLAYING. Accompanying techniques.

B. **Musicianship.**

    1. NOTATION. Simultaneous reading of piano score and song text.

C. **Bartók's Comments.** Sing and play the piece. Compare it to speech. In order to emphasize the ability of expression of music—contrary to the opinion of post-war years—interrogatory and answering verses have been put to the respective sections of the melody. It is recommended that the piece be sung by two pupils (or two groups of pupils) alternatively before practising it.

D. **Suggestions.** The piece can be performed in a variety of ways: pupil and teacher can alternate the singing of its phrases, the teacher can accompany the pupil's singing, and the pupil can accompany himself.

No. 15.   Village Song.

A. **Technique.**

    1. TOUCH. **Legato.**

    2. POSITION. Five-note range in four positions.

    3. FINGERING PROBLEMS. Black key playing.

B. **Musicianship.**

    1. NOTATION. Bartók-devised key signature. Accidentals.

    2. EXPRESSION.

        (a) Phrasing: ternary form.

C. **Bartók's Comments.** First study with a title. It is a sort of *G* major with altered fourth. A parallel can be found in the **Sarabande** from the First Partita of J. S. Bach. Asymmetrical phrase structure.

D. **Suggestions.** Note the metronome mark. Compare the form and phrase structure of this piece with that of no. 13.

No. 16.   Parallel Motion and Change of Position.

A. **Technique.**

   1. TOUCH. **Legato.**

   2. POSITION. Five-note range in two positions.

B. **Musicianship.**

   1. NOTATION. Reading of two voices which proceed in the same direction at the interval of a tenth.

   2. RHYTHM. Syncopation.

C. **Bartók's Comments.** Irregularity and variety of structure. Key of *C*.

D. **Suggestions.** Accent slightly the half notes in m. 20, and

note the contrary motion between M. 21 and 22.

No. 17.   Contrary Motion.

A. **Technique.**

   1. TOUCH. **Legato.**

   2. HAND INDEPENDENCE.

     (a) Counterpoint.

   3. FINGERING PROBLEMS. Black key playing L.H. only.

B. **Musicianship.**

   1. NOTATION. Accidentals.

   2. RHYTHM. Syncopation.

   3. EXPRESSION.

     (a) Phrasing: symmetrical phrases in ternary form.

C. **Bartók's Comments.** Same dissonance can be observed in Bach. This melody used in no. 13.

D. **Suggestions.** Accent slightly the half notes in M. 3, 7 and 15.

Nos. 18-21. Four Unison Melodies.

A. **Technique.**
   1. TOUCH. **Legato.**
   2. FINGERING PROBLEMS. Extension of the hand in the playing of various melodic intervals.

B. **Musicianship.**
   1. NOTATION. The whole rest. The separating sign | which indicates the interruption of **legato** between phrases.[1]
   2. EXPRESSION.
      (a) Dynamics: the **marcato** (>) accent.

C. **Bartók's Comments.** The melodies stress interval playing. Use the exercises to explain them. No. 20 combines intervals and change of direction. No. 21 is in *A* minor; it introduces accents.

D. **Suggestions.** Play nos. 18-20 as one unit, and Ex. 1a-c. No. 21 is concerned with the playing of accents. Practise Ex. 1d-f with no. 21.

In no. 20, the second phrase is extended by the addition of a measure of rest, and the fourth phrase is extended by the addition of the tied whole note. The use of these contrasting types of additions serves to extend asymmetrical phrases into balanced structures.

The accents appearing in no. 21 call for slight intensification of the notes they modify, and they should be played without hand motion (that is, with the fingers only). What is the purpose of | in m. 8?[1] The sign also serves as a warning that the following measures require alternate motion of the hands. The pianist, because of his or her preoccupation with the playing of accents, may overlook the ties and rests in the last three measures.

No. 22. Imitation and Counterpoint.

A. **Technique.**
   1. TOUCH. **Legato.**
   2. HAND INDEPENDENCE.
      (a) Counterpoint.

B. **Musicianship.**
   1. NOTATION. Reading of treble clef notation in L.H.
   2. EXPRESSION.
      (a) Dynamics: *f.*

---

1 See p. 15 for explanation.

C. **Bartók's Comments.** Similar voices in contrapuntal style. Imitation: the second voice commences later and is similar to the first voice. *G* tonality.

D. **Suggestions.** This piece is more difficult to play than no. 23. It may be advisable, therefore, to reverse the order of pieces and perform no. 23 together with Ex. 2 as the first examples of polyphonic playing.

Be sure that all rests are observed, and that the re-entry of one voice does not interrupt the flow of **legato** in the other voice. Observe also that *f* = **forte** = loud, and that counterpoint is the simultaneous playing of two or more independent melodic lines.

No. 23. Imitation and Inversion.

  A. **Technique.**

    1. TOUCH. **Legato**

    2. HAND INDEPENDENCE.
      (a) Counterpoint.

  B. **Musicianship.**

    1. NOTATION. Reading of individual melodic lines with bass clef notation in L.H.

    2. EXPRESSION.
      (a) Dynamics: *f.*

C. **Bartók's Comments.** One voice imitates the other and then inverts. Inversion: the position of the (two) voices is so changed that the upper voice becomes the lower and vice-versa (bars 1, 2, 3, and 7, 8, 9 show the original position, the remaining bars show the inversion).

D. **Suggestions.** See no. 22, above.

No. 24. Pastorale.

  A. **Technique.**

    1. TOUCH. **Legato.**

    2. FINGERING PROBLEMS. Black key playing.

  B. **Musicianship.**

    1. NOTATION. Whole rest in 3/4 time. *A* key signature.

    2. RHYTHM. Syncopation.

3. EXPRESSION.
    (a) Dynamics: **p** = **piano** = soft.
    (b) Phrasing: the last measure is added for structural
        balance. Ternary form.

  C. **Bartók's Comments.** Key of *D* with *g♯* added for practical
purposes.

  D. **Suggestions.** In the Lydian Mode built from *D* as principal
tone. Do not interrupt the flow of **legato** at the junction of phrases
in m. 7.

No. 25. Imitation and Inversion.

  A. **Technique.**

    1. TOUCH. **Legato.**

    2. HAND INDEPENDENCE.
      (a) Counterpoint.

  B. **Musicianship.**

    1. NOTATION. Bartók-devised key signature. The whole
      rest in 2/4 time. Repeat signs ‖: :‖ .

    2. RHYTHM. 2/4.

    3. EXPRESSION.
      (a) Tempo: M.M. = 150.
      (b) Dynamics: *sf* = **sforzato** (or **sforzando**) = very loud
        accent.

  C. **Bartók's Comments.** *B* minor feeling with lowered fifth.
Asymmetrical in form. The signature is *C♯*. See Notes.

  D. **Suggestions.** Review the meaning of the various types of
accent marks used in the **Mikrokosmos** (see p. 24). The tempo may
be too rapid for certain pianists. In such cases, the composer advises
a reduction in speed (see Preface to **Mikrokosmos**).

No. 26. Repetition.

A. **Technique.**

1. TOUCH. **Legato** and **non-legato.**

2. HAND INDEPENDENCE.
   (a) Counterpoint.
   (b) Combined Touch-Forms: **legato** vs. **non-legato.**

B. **Musicianship.**

NOTATION. D key signature.

C. **Bartók's Comments.** Second voice repeats first voice in sequence in rhythmic form beginning on the dominant. Has the character of D major, ending on the fifth degree in the L.H. and the second degree in the R.H. This is called a half-cadence, frequently used in Yugoslav music.

D. **Suggestions.** There may be some difficulty in playing this piece at the indicated tempo. The repeated notes played in one hand must not interrupt the **legato** playing in the other hand. Play Ex. 3 as a preparation for no. 27.

No. 27. Syncopation.

A. **Technique.**

1. TOUCH. **Legato.**

2. HAND INDEPENDENCE.
   (a) Counterpoint.

3. FINGERING PROBLEMS. Black key playing.

B. **Musicianship.**

1. RHYTHM. Syncopation.

C. **Bartók's Comments.** Asymmetrical phrase structure. Tied-over syncopation. Same melody used in no. 9.

D. **Suggestions.** Review the meaning of counterpoint by comparing nos. 9 and 27.

No. 28. Canon at the Octave.

A. **Technique.**

1. TOUCH. **Legato.**

2. HAND INDEPENDENCE.
   (a) Counterpoint.

B. **Musicianship.**

1. RHYTHM. Syncopation.
2. EXPRESSION.
   (a) Dynamics: *p.*
   (b) Phrasing: in canonic form.

C. **Bartók's Comments.** Canon: two equal voices are introduced so that one commences later than the other. There can be any interval between the voices. In no. 28 it is an octave, hence the title "Canon at the Octave." *E* minor with altered second. Same melody used in no. 7.

D. **Suggestions.** Compare this piece with no. 7 to illustrate the explanation of canonic form. Syncopated notes should be accented slightly. Note the dynamic level. Practise Ex. 4 as a preparation for no. 29.

No. 29. Imitation Reflected.

A. **Technique.**

1. TOUCH. **Legato.**
2. HAND INDEPENDENCE.
   (a) Counterpoint.
3. FINGERING PROBLEMS. Black key playing in R.H.

B. **Musicianship.**

NOTATION. Accidentals.

C. **Bartók's Comments.** Seven-bar sections. Direct mirror-like reflection of the first voice. Imitation reflected: the melodic line of the imitating (lower) voice runs in contrary direction to that of the upper voice.

D. **Suggestions.** The flow of **legato** between phrases must not be interrupted.

No. 30. Canon at the Lower Fifth.

A. **Technique.**

1. TOUCH. **Legato** and **non-legato.**
2. HAND INDEPENDENCE.
   (a) Counterpoint.
   (b) Combined Touch-Forms: **Legato** vs. **non-legato.**

B. **Musicianship.**

    1. RHYTHM. Syncopation.

    2. EXPRESSION.

      (a) Tempo: **moderato** = at a moderate rate of speed.

      (b) Phrasing: in canonic form.

C. **Bartók's Comments.** Intervals and direction of the two voices are the same, but the interval between them is different. See note to no. 28. The interval of the two voices is here a fifth.

D. **Suggestions.** The repeated notes in one hand must not interrupt the **legato** playing in the other hand. First tempo indication.

No. 31. Little Dance in Canon Form.

A. **Technique.**

    1. TOUCH. **Legato** and **non-legato.**

    2. HAND INDEPENDENCE.

      (a) Counterpoint.

      (b) Combined Touch-Forms: **legato** vs. **non-legato.**

      (c) Dynamic Contrast: > vs. *f.*

B. **Musicianship.**

    1. NOTATION. The repeat sign.

    2. EXPRESSION.

      (a) Tempo: **allegro** = quick, brisk. M.M. = 160.

      (b) Dynamics: **marcato** accents in each hand.

      (c) Phrasing: in canonic form.

C. **Bartók's Comments.** An identical canon in pitch and interval.

D. **Suggestions.** First example in which the voices are contrasted dynamically. It is more important to acquire control of accents than to attempt the playing of this piece at the indicated tempo.

No. 32. In Dorian Mode.

A. **Technique.**

    1. TOUCH. **Legato.**

    2. HAND INDEPENDENCE.

      (a) Counterpoint.

    3. INTERVAL AND BROKEN CHORD PLAYING. L.H. only.

    4. FINGERING PROBLEMS.

B. **Musicianship.**

   1. NOTATION. The dotted whole note in 3/2 time. The dotted line between staves.

   2. RHYTHM. Subdivision of the beat into two parts, the half note as the pulse unit.

   3. EXPRESSION.

      (a) Tempo: **Lento** = slow.

      (b) Terms: **legato** = in a smooth and connected manner, with no break between the tones.

   C. **Bartók's Comments.** Dorian Mode: One of the so-called ecclesiastical modes. Beginning on *D* as principal tone the degrees of this scale have no accidentals (there are white keys only).

Built from C as principal tone the scale should read as follows:

   Therefore, it is a minor (minor third) scale with a major sixth and a minor seventh. This and the following ecclesiastical modes were used in the middle ages until about the 17th century but, since J. S. Bach, they have been replaced in Art music by the major and minor scales. However, besides many other unnamed scales, they are still flourishing in the folk music of Eastern Europe (Hungary, Rumania, Yugoslavia, etc.) and Asia and are not at all antiquated.

   This piece has a major chord ending as in Bach.

   D. **Suggestions.** In M. 7 and 12, *g* is played with the first finger

of each hand.

In m. 6, the dotted line indicates that *f* (played by the L.H.) is a continuation of the melody in the R.H.

A solid line would indicate the

playing of that note with the R.H. Take notice of the metronome mark: it indicates rate of speed of the quarter note and does not affect conception of the half note as the pulse unit (count *one and two and three and* in each measure). See **Suggestions** in no. 33, below.

No. 33.   Slow Dance.

   A. **Technique.**

      1. TOUCH. **Legato.**

      2. HAND INDEPENDENCE.
        (a) Counterpoint.

      3. FINGERING PROBLEMS. Black key playing in L.H. only.

   B. **Musicianship.**

      1. NOTATION. The dotted whole note in 6/4 time. Bass clef leger-line notes above the staff.

      2. RHYTHM. 6/4. Syncopation.

      3. EXPRESSION.
        (a) Tempo: **Andante** = moving, walking.
        (b) Dynamics: *mf* = **mezzo forte** = softer than **forte** (half-loud). < = **crescendo** = increasing gradually in loudness.

   C. **Bartók's Comments.** *G* tonality, c♯ gives color in contemporary music. Ends on a half-cadence.

   D. **Suggestions.** 3/2 is a simple triple meter accented as follows:

$\frac{3}{2}$ ♩ ♩ ♩ ♩ ♩ ♩ | . On the other hand, 6/4 is a com-

pound duple meter: $\frac{6}{4}$ ♩ ♩ ♩ ♩ ♩ ♩ |

Note the difference between these time signatures in terms of accentuation and counting, and their similarity with reference to notation. It is recommended that the pianist demonstrate his under-standing by playing no. 32 in 6/4 and no. 33 in 3/2. In the last two measures, the marks in parenthesis illustrate the function of the **crescendo** mark $<$.

No. 34. In Phrygian Mode.

    A. **Technique.**

        1. TOUCH. **Legato.**

        2. HAND INDEPENDENCE.

            (a) Counterpoint.

            (b) Dynamic Contrast: *sf* vs. *f.*

    B. **Musicianship.**

        1. RHYTHM. Subdivision of the beat into two parts: the half note as the pulse unit. Syncopation.

        2. EXPRESSION.

            (a) Tempo: **Calmo** = moderate.

            (b) Dynamics: **cresc.** = **crescendo; dim.** = **diminuendo** = becoming gradually softer.

    C. **Bartók's Comments.** Phrygian Mode: One of the ecclesiastical modes beginning on *E* as principal tone with seven degrees without accidentals (a minor scale with a minor second, sixth and seventh).

Tonal and rhythmic variety within a short range. 2/2 meter. This modal style used in Hungary for the last 150 years.

    D. **Suggestions.** In the last four measures, the dynamic marks in parenthesis illustrate the function of the **diminuendo (dim.)** mark.

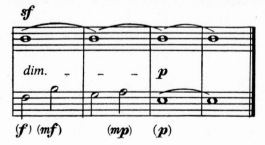

No. 35.   Chorale.

A. **Technique.**
>   1. TOUCH. **Legato.**
>   2. HAND INDEPENDENCE.
>   (a) Counterpoint.

B. **Musicianship.**
>   1. EXPRESSION.
>   (a) Tempo. **Largamente** = slow (broadly, largely).

C. **Bartók's Comments.** Voices resemble free canon writing.

D. **Suggestions.** Chorale = a hymn tune of the German Protestant Church. There seems to be a certain similarity between this piece and a chorale, particularly in terms of construction.

No. 36.   Free Canon.

A. **Technique.**
>   1. TOUCH. **Legato.**
>   2. INDEPENDENCE.
>   (a) Counterpoint.

B. **Musicianship.**
>   1. EXPRESSION.
>   (a) Tempo: **Teneramente** = (tenderly, delicately) moderate
>   in speed.

C. **Bartók's Comments.** See note for no. 28. The canon is "free" if the second voice deviates inconsiderably from the first. Natural *A* minor.

D. **Suggestions.** Do not overlook the quarter rests in M. 3-10. **Péteré** (printed parallel to the double bar) indicates that Bartók has dedicated Volume I of the **Mikrokosmos** to his second son, Peter.

No. 37. In Lydian Mode.

  A. **Technique.**

    1. TOUCH. **Legato, non-legato** and **tenuto.**

    2. HAND INDEPENDENCE.
      (a) Counterpoint.

  B. **Musicianship.**

    1. NOTATION. The eighth note and rest in 2/4. ⌢ =
    fermata = pause, hold.

    2. RHYTHM. Subdivision of the beat into two parts: the
    quarter note as the pulse unit.

    3. EXPRESSION.
      (a) Tempo: **Allegretto** = slower than **allegro,** moderately
      fast.

  C. **Bartók's Comments.** Lydian Mode: Another ecclesiastical
mode beginning on *F* as principal tone with 7 degrees without
accidentals, a major scale with augmented fourth. This interval is so
characteristic in this scale that a melody based on the first five degrees
only (as no. 37) may be called "Lydian."

Direct imitation in voices. Ends on dominant.

  D. **Suggestions. Tenuto** touch: the key is pressed rather than
struck down. The **fermata** "about doubles the value of the note
beneath it." Prepare Ex. 5.

No. 38. Staccato and Legato.

  A. **Technique.**

    1. TOUCH. **Legato** and **staccato.**

    2. HAND INDEPENDENCE.
      (a) Counterpoint.
      (b) Combined Touch-Forms: **legato** vs. **staccato.**

B. **Musicianship.**
  1. NOTATION. *D* key signature. **Staccato** signs.
  2. RHYTHM. Subdivision of the beat into two parts: the quarter note as the pulse unit in 3/4.

C. **Bartók's Comments.** The signature is not conventional. Develops ability to play **staccato** and **legato.** Voices are reflected. See exercise in appendix.

D. **Suggestions.** Note the hand independence required in m. 7.

Staccato tones should be sounded for "one-half the value of the note (or less)."

No. 39. Staccato and Legato.

A. **Technique.**
  1. TOUCH. **Legato** and **staccato.**
  2. HAND INDEPENDENCE.
     (a) Counterpoint.
     (b) Combined Touch-Forms: **legato** vs. **staccato.**

B. **Musicianship.**
  1. NOTATION. *F* key signature.
  2. RHYTHM. Subdivision of the beat into two parts: the quarter note as the pulse unit in 4/4.
  3. EXPRESSION.
     (a) Tempo: **Comodo** = at a convenient pace, leisurely.
     (b) Phrasing: in canonic form.

C. **Bartók's Comments.** Contrast of **staccato** and **legato** in each hand in contrapuntal style. Might be good to talk about different types of **staccato**—the shorter and longer types.[1]

D. **Suggestions.** The playing of **legato** vs. **staccato** may prove difficult. Slow practice is recommended. If Bartók's comment concerning the teaching of **staccato** types is followed, demonstrate how the piece would sound if played **staccatissimo.**

---
1 See page 14 for explanation.

No. 40. In Yugoslav Mode.

A. **Technique.**

   1. TOUCH. **Legato.**

   2. HAND INDEPENDENCE.

     (a) Accompanying Figurations: in L.H.

B. **Musicianship.**

   1. NOTATION. *A* key signature.

   2. EXPRESSION.

     (a) Dynamics: ∧ = **marcatissimo** accent = moderately
strong accent.

     (b) Phrasing: in ternary form.

     (c) Terms: **La seconda volta** = the second time.

C. **Bartók's Comments.** *E* Mixolydian Mode. Ends on half-cadence. Imitation of Yugoslav bagpipes: the piece is written for two pipes although the instrument has three. The Scotch bagpipe has only a chanter and a drone. The Yugoslav has three pipes: chanter, tonic-dominant, and drone (a tonic pipe). A bagpipe melody can be found in the main theme of Beethoven's Sixth Symphony.

D. **Suggestions.** Mixolydian Mode: An ecclesiastical mode beginning on *G* as principal tone with seven degrees without accidentals

(a major scale with a minor

seventh). Built from *E* as principal tone the scale should read as

follows:

Ending on the Dominant (V) has the same effect for the Yugoslav peasant as the ending on the tonic (I) has for those exposed to Western (Europe) art music.

Practise Ex. 6-8.

No. 41. Melody with Accompaniment.

A. **Technique.**

   1. TOUCH. **Legato.**

   2. HAND INDEPENDENCE.

     (a) Dynamic Contrast: *mf* vs. **p.**

     (b) Accompanying Figurations: in L.H.

3. BROKEN CHORD PLAYING. In L.H.

4. FINGER INDEPENDENCE. First example of part-playing in L.H.

B. **Musicianship.**

1. NOTATION. Bartók-devised key signature. The whole rest in 6/8.

2. RHYTHM. Change of meter. Subdivision of the beat into three parts: the dotted quarter as the pulse unit in 6/8 and 9/8.

3. EXPRESSION.
   (a) Tempo: **Adagio** = slow.
   (b) Terms: **sempre legato** = always **legato.** The use of this instruction eliminates the necessity of inserting **legato** slurs in the L.H.

C. **Bartók's Comments.** Changes in meter and rhythmic patterns. C♯ for key signature. Broken chords up and in reverse direction. G major with an augmented fourth and a minor seventh.

D. **Suggestions.** First example of Bartók's use of a compound mode consisting of G Mixolydian with the Lydian ♯4:

Observe the tied notes in the last two measures.

Count: *1 2 3 4 5 6   1 2 3 4 5 6*

No. 42. Accompaniment in Broken Triads.

A. **Technique.**

1. TOUCH. **Legato** and **staccato.**

2. HAND INDEPENDENCE.
   (a) Dynamic Contrast: **p** vs. **mf.**
   (b) Accompanying Figurations: in each hand.

3. BROKEN CHORD PLAYING. In each hand.

B. **Musicianship.**

    1. NOTATION. Leger-line notes below staff in treble clef.

    2. EXPRESSION.

        (a) Tempo: **Andante tranquillo** $=$ moving tranquilly, at a moderate rate of speed.

C. **Bartók's Comments.** Sustained theme in R.H., broken chords in L.H., then reversed. Chords are all practically the same but with a few altered or foreign tones.

D. **Suggestions.** In m. 14, the *c* in the R.H. is natural

and in m. 34 the *c* in the L.H. is also natural.

The effect is bitonal: major vs. minor with *A* as the

principal tone for both modes. Practise Ex. 9.

No. 43. In Hungarian Style.

A. **Technique.**

    1. TOUCH. **Legato** and **staccato.**

    2. HAND INDEPENDENCE.

        (a) Counterpoint.

    3. FINGERING PROBLEMS. Black key playing in Piano II.

    4. ENSEMBLE PLAYING. For two pianos, four hands.

B. **Musicianship.**

    1. NOTATION. Mixed accidentals and dotted notes. Bass clef notation in each hand.

    2. RHYTHM. The dotted quarter in 4/4.

    3. EXPRESSSION.

        (a) Terms: **più** $=$ more.

C. **Bartók's Comments.** First example of an arrangement for two pianos. Piano I plays broken thirds in parallel motion. See exercises in appendix. After the solo version "a" has been played, the second piano part of the same grade of difficulty which is provided may be added. Version "b" shows the melody written in conventional style. The theme is the same but the thirds are in contrary motion. *G* minor with augmented sixth.

D. **Suggestions.** Alternate the playing of both parts. If only one piano is available, transpose the **primo** (Piano I) part two octaves higher and play with another pianist as a duet for four hands. Hungarian style: the A A⁵ B A form of this piece is typical of Hungarian folk song structure.

Hungarian style: the A A^5 B A form of this piece is typical of Hungarian folk song structure.

No. 44. Contrary Motion.

A. **Technique.**
1. TOUCH. **Legato, staccato** and **tenuto.**
2. HAND INDEPENDENCE.
   (a) Counterpoint.
   (b) Combined Touch-Forms: **legato** vs. **staccato.**
3. ENSEMBLE PLAYING. For two pianos, four hands.

B. **Musicianship.**
1. NOTATION. Devised two-sharp signature in Piano I and *E* key signature in Piano II. Accidentals.
2. EXPRESSION.
   (a) Terms: **Vivace** = lively.

C. **Bartók's Comments.** Note the signature: key of *E* but additional sharps not added because they are not used. Ends with an augmented third in doubled notes. Can be played without the second piano part.

D. **Suggestions.** See **Suggestions** in no. 43 above.

No. 45. Méditation.

A. **Technique.**
1. TOUCH. **Legato, staccato** and **tenuto.**
2. HAND INDEPENDENCE.
   (a) Combined Touch-Forms: **legato** vs. **staccato** and **tenuto.**

     (b) Dynamic Contrast: *p* vs. *mf.*

     (c) Accompanying Figurations: in each hand.

  3. BROKEN CHORD PLAYING. In each hand.

  4. FINGERING PROBLEMS. Black key playing in each hand.

B. Musicianship

  1. NOTATION. E♮ key signature.

  2. EXPRESSION.

     (a) Dynamics: *mp* = **mezzo piano** = half-soft, louder than *p.*

     (b) Terms: **subito** = suddenly.

C. Bartók's Comments. Although signature of piece is *C* minor, the composition is in *F* minor with a major sixth. Abstract in theme and rhythm. Returns to former Dorian Mode. Can be played on two pianos, the second player executing the same piece on the higher octave.

D. Suggestions. Check

fingering in M. 11-12.

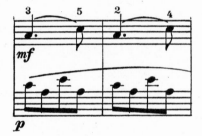

The *d* is natural in M. 14-16.

No. 46. Increasing—Diminishing.

  A. **Technique.**

    1. TOUCH. **Legato.**

    2. HAND INDEPENDENCE.

     (a) Counterpoint.

     (b) Dynamic Contrasts: *mf* vs. *p*, *f* vs. *mf*, *pp* vs. *p.*

B. **Musicianship.**

   1. RHYTHM. Syncopation.

   2. EXPRESSION.

     (a) Dynamics: *pp* = **pianissimo** = softer than *p.*

C. **Bartók's Comments.** Tone control. Not for the average pupil.

D. **Suggestions.** Phrygian Mode, ending on the dominant. Double bar in m. 14 indicates the midpoint of this piece in terms of dynamic level. Key speed is the determining factor in dynamics: fast key descent will produce a loud tone and slow key descent will result in a soft tone. Prepare Ex. 10-11.

No. 47. Big Fair.

A. **Technique.**

   1. TOUCH. **Non-legato.**

   2. HAND INDEPENDENCE.

     (a) Counterpoint.

     (b) Dynamic Contrasts: *sf* and ∧ vs. *f.*

     (c) Accompanying Figurations: L.H. only.

   3. PEDALLING. Use of the damper pedal.

   4. FINGERING PROBLEMS. 'Discontinuous' fingerings.

B. **Musicianship.**

   1. NOTATION. *G* key signature.

   2. RHYTHM. Subdivision of the beat into two parts: the half note as the pulse unit in 2/2.

   3. EXPRESSION.

     (a) Tempo: **con brio** = with spirit. M.M. = 132.

     (b) Phrasing: in ternary form.

     (c) Terms: **strepitoso** = noisily; **sempre simile** = in like manner throughout; **senza** = without; **Ped.** = depress the damper pedal; **meno** = less; ✳ = release the damper pedal.

C. **Bartók's Comments.** Voices moving in broken thirds and fourths in contrary motion which creates an atmosphere of excitement. Use of the pedal and shading very important.

D. **Suggestions.** One of the difficult pieces in this volume; in fact, the combination of pedalling, accentuation, and discontinuity of fingering may be beyond the ability of some students at the indicated tempo.

No. 48.   In Mixolydian Mode.

A. **Technique.**
1. TOUCH. **Legato.**
2. HAND INDEPENDENCE.
   (a) Counterpoint.
   (b) Dynamic Contrast: *mf* vs. *f.*
   (c) Accompanying Figurations: in each hand.
3. BROKEN CHORD PLAYING. In each hand.

B. **Musicianship.**
1. RHYTHM. 5/4. Syncopation.
2. EXPRESSION.
   (a) Tempo: **Allegro non troppo** = not too fast.

C. **Bartók's Comments.** Key of *G* with no accidentals. Mixolydian Mode: an ecclesiastical mode with *G* as principal tone and seven degrees without accidentals. Ends on dominant. L.H. figures in broken chords or chord of *G* with foreign notes. Chord in *E* minor. R.H. melody in contrary motion. Very good for individual finger control. I checked all the **Mikrokosmos** pieces against the metronome.

D. **Suggestions.** Accent slightly the first beat of each measure of accompanying figurations as well as the syncopated notes. Observe the dynamic changes in the last five measures.

No. 49.   Crescendo-Diminuendo.

A. **Technique.**
1. TOUCH. **Legato** and **staccato.**
2. HAND INDEPENDENCE.
   (a) Counterpoint.
   (b) Combined Touch-Forms: **legato** vs. **staccato.**

B. **Musicianship.**
1. NOTATION. Mixed accidentals.
2. EXPRESSION.
   (a) Dynamics: as indicated by the title.

C. **Bartók's Comments.** Quick change from **legato** to **staccato.** Key of *C* with accidentals. **Crescendo** and **diminuendo.**

D. **Suggestions.** Practise first without dynamics at M.M. ♪= 96-160. Then play at indicated tempo and intensities.

No. 50. Minuetto.

A. **Technique.**

    1. TOUCH. **Legato** and **staccato.**

    2. HAND INDEPENDENCE.
        (a) Counterpoint.
        (b) Combined Touch-Forms: **legato** vs. **staccato.**

B. **Musicianship.**

    1. NOTATION. Devised one-sharp key signature.

    2. EXPRESSION.
        (a) Tempo: **Tempo di Menuetto** = at the speed of a
            minuet. The minuet dates from about the end of the
            17th Century and it is a slow, stately dance in triple
            meter.
        (b) Phrasing: in ternary form.
        (c) Dynamics: $>$ = gradually get softer.

    C. **Bartók's Comments.** Application of **staccato** and **legato** play-ing. Key of *A* major with altered tones.

    D. **Suggestions.** Compound mode: *A* Major with the Lydian augmented fourth.

Check the playing of **legato** (R.H.) vs. **staccato** (L.H.) in the last two measures.

No. 51. Waves.

A. **Technique.**

    1. TOUCH. **Legato** and **espressivo.**

    2. HAND INDEPENDENCE.
        (a) Counterpoint.

    3. FINGERING PROBLEMS. Black key playing.

B. **Musicianship.**

  1. NOTATION. $D\flat$ key signature.

  2. RHYTHM. The upbeat and syncopation in 6/8.

  3. EXPRESSION.
    (a) Tempo: **poco ritard.** = growing a little slower.
    (b) Dynamics: **p subito** = suddenly soft.

C. **Bartók's Comments.** Good demonstration of the tie on different beats in one voice while the other voice proceeds. Key of $D\flat$ ending on dominant. Imitation of voices: one in the tonic and one in the dominant. Can be played on two pianos, the second player executing the same piece in the higher octave.

D. **Suggestions.** Bitonal: upper voice in $A\flat$ and lower voice in $D\flat$. To play **dolce,** use pressure touch (**tenuto**) combined with flexible wrist action (without weight) so that percussiveness is reduced to a minimum.

Note the **decrescendo** marks above the slurred notes in R.H. of M. 14-15.

A more appropriate English title for this piece would be "Vacillation" (unsteady swaying), according to Bartók's original Hungarian title.

No. 52.   Unison Divided.

A. **Technique.**

  1. TOUCH. **Legato, non-legato,** and **tenuto:** from hand to hand.

B. **Musicianship.**

  1. EXPRESSION.
    (a) Dynamics: **cresc.** and > .

C. **Bartók's Comments.** Melody is divided between the hands. Key of G with altered fourths.

D. **Suggestions.** Compound mode: *G* Mixolydian with Lydian ♯4.[2] There may be a tendency to play **legatissimo** when changing from hand to hand, or to play **legato** in the second and last measures. Notes in bass and treble clefs are to be played with L.H. and R.H. respectively.

No. 53.   In Transylvanian Style.

A. **Technique.**

    1. TOUCH. **Legato, non-legato** and **tenuto:** from hand to hand.

    2. HAND INDEPENDENCE.
      (a) Counterpoint.

B. **Musicianship.**

    1. NOTATION. Clef changes.

    2. RHYTHM. Subdivision of the beat into two and four parts: the half note as the pulse unit in 2/2. Syncopation.

    3. EXPRESSION.
      (a) Tempo: **Risoluto** = energetic, with decision.

C. **Bartók's Comments.** Imitation of R.H. in L.H. Continuity from one hand to the other expresses one idea. Note changes in clef signs and hand positions. Key of *D.*

D. **Suggestions.** Subdivision of the beat into four parts through use of the eighth note in 2/2 meter. The eighth notes can be counted:

m. 3

Count: *1 a and a   2 a and a*

Dotted lines indicate the melody is taken up by L.H. Note the separating sign in L.H. of m. 24. Transylvania is an area formerly part of Hungary, comprised mainly of Rumanian peasantry, lying to the east of Hungary and north of Rumania. Bartók collected folk music in Transylvania in the decade prior to its assignment to Rumania in 1920 by the Treaty of Trianon.

See 41 D. for illustration.

This piece is built on
the pattern:

which Bartók discovered to be a typical rhythmic structure of
Transylvanian instrumental melodies.

No. 54.   Chromatic.

A. **Technique.**
  1. TOUCH. **Legato** and **staccato.**
  2. HAND INDEPENDENCE.
     (a) Counterpoint.
  3. FINGERING PROBLEMS. Chromatics.

B. **Musicianship.**
  1. NOTATION. Accidentals.
  2. EXPRESSION.
     (a) Dynamics.

C. **Bartók's Comments.** Chromatic study with quick, forceful,
and sudden **staccato.** Definite shading and accents. Good place to
take up the chromatic scale if the pupil hasn't had it. (See no. 91 D.)

D. **Suggestions.** Be sure to observe the rests on b. 1 of M. 3, 6
and 11. Awkward hand contraction in M. 9-10 may call for extra

practice. Bartók's original
title, **Crescendo-Diminuendo,**
indicates the importance of
perfecting dynamic shadings
here. Prepare Ex. 12-13.

No. 55.   Triplets in Lydian Mode.

A. **Technique.**
  1. TOUCH. **Legato** and **staccato.**
  2. HAND INDEPENDENCE.
     (a) Counterpoint.
     (b) Dynamic Contrast: **in relievo** = bring out, in relief.
     (c) Accompanying Figurations: **staccato** intervals in each
         hand.
  3. INTERVAL PLAYING. Fifths.
  4. ENSEMBLE PLAYING. For two pianos, four hands.

B. **Musicianship.**

1. NOTATION. Clef changes (**secondo** only).

2. RHYTHM. Subdivision of the beat into three parts: the quarter note as the pulse unit in 3/4. Polyrhythm: the simultaneous combination of two to the beat (in one part) vs. three to the beat (in the other part). Change of time.

3. EXPRESSION.
(a) Tempo: **Tempo di marcia** = in march time.

C. **Bartók's Comments.** Consult exercises in appendix before playing this piece. Consecutive fifths used: avoided yesterday, used today. See notes for nos. 37 and 44. The accidentals are used for color, although this mode has none. L.H. is the metronome since it keeps the beat steady.

D. **Suggestions.** Bring out the melody in L.H. of M. 9-15 (in Piano I) as indicated.
In the same part, because of the change from 2/4 to 3/4 at m. 17, the pianist may interpolate a quarter rest between M. 17 and 18.

in rilievo

Play both parts. If only one piano is available, another performer can play the **secondo** part transposed an octave down (M. 10-15 transposed two octaves down). Practise Ex. 14 as preparation for the part-playing to be encountered in no. 56, making sure that the ties are observed when repeating each two-measure section or when proceeding from one section to another.

No. 56. Melody in Tenths.

A. **Technique.**
 1. TOUCH. **Legato.**
 2. FINGER INDEPENDENCE. Part-playing in each hand.

B. **Musicianship.**
 1. NOTATION. Treble clef in each hand.
 2. EXPRESSION.
 (a) Dynamics.

C. **Bartók's Comments.** Two voices are sustained while others move. Ends on a consonant chord. In old music a chord built of consecutive thirds, even with the seventh degree added. was called a consonant chord. At first the chord contained a major third, but later one with a minor third was also considered to be consonant. Can be played on two pianos, the second player executing the piece in the higher octave.

D. **Suggestions.** As a preparation for part-playing, Bartók recommends use of both hands in playing the individual line systems of one staff. If this is done, the fingerings should be rearranged to avoid awkward juxtaposition of the hands. When the piece is played as written, be sure the held tones are maintained throughout each phrase. Note the alternation of modes: Aeolian to Dorian to Phrygian, each with *A* as the principal tone.

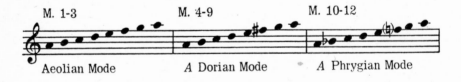

M. 1-3   M. 4-9   M. 10-12

Aeolian Mode   *A* Dorian Mode   *A* Phrygian Mode

No. 57. Accents.

A. **Technique.**
 1. TOUCH. **Non-legato.**
 2. HAND INDEPENDENCE.
 (a) Counterpoint.
 (b) Dynamic Contrasts: > vs. *p,* *mf* and *f.* ∧ vs. *f* and *ff.*
 3. POSITION. Hand crossings: L.H. over, R.H. under.
 4. FINGER INDEPENDENCE. Part-playing in each hand.

B. **Musicianship.**

    1. NOTATION. Change of signature: key of *C*, *A*, and *E*. Change of clef.

    2. RHYTHM. Subdivision of the beat into two and four parts: the half note as the pulse unit in 2/2. Syncopation.

    3. EXPRESSION.

        (a) Tempo: **Non troppo vivo** = not too lively.

        (b) Dynamics: **molto marcato** = very marked, accented.

        (c) Phrasing: Canonic writing in variation form.

  C. **Bartók's Comments.** Accents on upbeats. Notice changes of keys and positions. Feeling is key of *A* in which the piece begins and ends, but the tonality is indefinite. Requires very good control for the accentuation.

  D. **Suggestions.** In the L.H. of M. 6 and 12, the separating sign

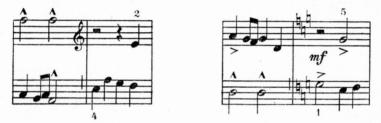

indicates the end of the phrase and that the half note preceding the sign can be shortened to allow for the quick change of position in M. 7 and 13. Another of the more difficult pieces in this volume. Play Ex. 15.

No. 58. In Oriental Style.

  A. **Technique.**

    1. TOUCH. **Espressivo.**

    2. HAND INDEPENDENCE.

        (a) Counterpoint.

  B. **Musicianship.**

    1. NOTATION. Change of clef (L.H. only).

    2. EXPRESSION.

        (a) Tempo: **Assai lento** = very slow, but not as slow as the indication **molto lento.**

        (b) Phrasing: the comma. In ternary form.

C. **Bartók's Comments.** *G* minor tonality typical of Oriental style contains a minor third and an augmented fourth. Ends on a half cadence. See exercise in appendix.

D. **Suggestions.** To be played with **espressivo** touch (see **Suggestions** of no. 51 above). The comma in the treble clef of m. 7

indicates a "slight, almost unnoticeable

pause". In this case, the time for separation should be taken from the note preceding the comma. Thus, m. 7 can be thought as consisting of a half note and a quarter rest.

In 1913, Bartók collected Arabic folk music in North Africa. Characteristics of this music, he found, are a melody formed of continuously-repeated motives of relatively few neighboring tones which include the interval of the augmented second, and 6/8 meter.

No. 59.   Major and Minor.

A. **Technique.**
   1. TOUCH. **Legato.**
   2. HAND INDEPENDENCE.
      (a) Counterpoint.
      (b) Dynamic Contrasts: ∧ , > , and *sf* vs. *f.*

B. **Musicianship.**
   1. NOTATION. The reading of accidentals involved in the simultaneous performance of *F* minor and *F* Lydian Modes.

C. **Bartók's Comments.** Contrasting minor in one part and major with alterations in the other. Could discuss here varieties of minor modes.

D. **Suggestions.** Play the various minor and major modes below and note carefully the characteristic key signatures and intervals of each.

MINOR MODES

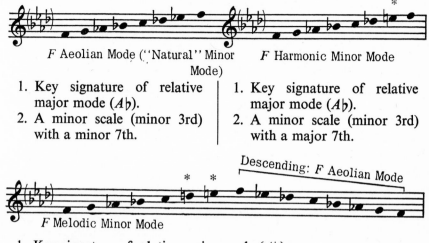

F Aeolian Mode ("Natural" Minor Mode)   F Harmonic Minor Mode

1. Key signature of relative major mode (*A*♭).
2. A minor scale (minor 3rd) with a minor 7th.

1. Key signature of relative major mode (*A*♭).
2. A minor scale (minor 3rd) with a major 7th.

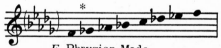

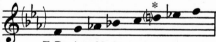

Descending: *F* Aeolian Mode

F Melodic Minor Mode

1. Key signature of relative major mode (*A*♭).
2. **Ascending:** a minor scale (minor 3rd) with a major 6th and a major 7th.
   Descending: the Aeolian Mode.

F Dorian Mode

1. Key signature one flat less (one sharp more) than relative major mode.
2. A minor scale (minor 3rd) with a major 6th.

F Phrygian Mode

1. Key signature one flat more (one sharp less) than relative major mode.
2. A minor scale (minor 3rd) with a minor 2nd.

MAJOR MODES

F Major Mode

1. Key signature of one flat (*B*♭).
2. Based on the stepwise[3] formula (building upwards from the first degree): S, S, ½S,   S, S, S, ½S

2½ steps   3½ steps

---

3 A half-step is the distance between two adjacent tones which have no white or black keys between them.

F Lydian Mode	*F* Mixolydian Mode
1. Key signature one flat less (one sharp more) than the **parallel** major (*F*).	1. Key signature one flat more (one sharp less) than the **parallel** major (*F*).
2. A major scale (major 3rd) with an augmented 4th.	2. A major scale (major 3rd) with a minor 7th.

No. 60. Canon with Sustained Notes.

   A. **Technique.**

       1. TOUCH. **Legato** and **non-legato.**

       2. FINGER INDEPENDENCE. Part-playing in each hand.

   B. **Musicianship.**

       1. NOTATION. *E* key signature.

       2. RHYTHM. 1/2 meter. Change of time.

       3. EXPRESSION.

          (a) Tempo: **Grave** = slow, serious, heavy.

          (b) Phrasing: in canonic form.

   C. **Bartók's Comments.** Play carefully so that the sustained notes are heard. Four-voice canon in 2/2 and 1/2 meter. In *E*.

   D. **Suggestions.** The separating signs here also indicate phrase endings. 1/2 meter = one beat in the measure, the half-note receives one beat.

No. 61. Pentatonic Melody.

   A. **Technique.**

       1. TOUCH. **Legato.**

       2. HAND INDEPENDENCE.

          (a) Dynamic Contrast: **in relievo.**

          (b) Accompanying Figurations: in each hand.

   B. **Musicianship.**

       1. NOTATION. Change of clef in L.H.

C. **Bartók's Comments.** Pentatonic: The scientific name is "anhemitone-pentatonic," that means a scale of five degrees without any semitone, or a minor scale where the second and sixth are missing. It was used frequently in the old Christian monodic ecclesiastical music and is still living in three centers: with the American Indians, with the African Negroes, and in Central Asia—which is the most important one. Each of these centers built different types upon the same basis. The Central Asian center spread its influence as far west as the Hungarians, eastwards to the Chinese and southwards to the Turks. The character of no. 61 resembles the Central Asian type. There are many kinds of pentatonic scales, some are in major. This is in the key of *A* minor although it ends on tonic and dominant fifths of *C*, a common ending in old music.

D. **Suggestions.** Prepare Ex. 16.

No. 62. Minor Sixths in Parallel Motion.

A. **Technique.**
1. TOUCH. **Legato, staccato,** and **tenuto.**
2. HAND INDEPENDENCE.
   (a) Counterpoint.
   (b) Dynamic Contrasts: > vs. *f.*
3. FINGER INDEPENDENCE. Part-playing in L.H. (m. 40).

B. **Musicianship.**
1. NOTATION. Mixed accidentals. Clef changes in L.H.
2. EXPRESSION.
   (a) Tempo: **Vivace, ma non troppo, risoluto** = resolutely but not too lively.
   (b) Dynamics: **marcato.**

C. **Bartók's Comments.** Gives impression of duo- or bitonality. Oriental feelings. Can be harmonized—see example in appendix.

D. **Suggestions.** Note juxtaposition of hands in m. 23. Strict

observance of eighth rests also will contribute to accuracy in terms of providing time needed to make the quick leaps in M. 24, 26, and 38. Note the separating signs in m.6: the second quarter

note should be played **staccato** but with **tenuto** touch.

No. 63. Buzzing.

A. **Technique.**

1. TOUCH. **Legato.**

2. HAND INDEPENDENCE.
   (a) Counterpoint.

3. FINGER INDEPENDENCE. Part-playing in L.H. (M. 1-2).

4. EMBELLISHMENTS. Slow trills in each hand.

B. **Musicianship.**

1. RHYTHM. Syncopation.

2. EXPRESSION.
   (a) Tempo: **con moto** = with animation, energetic movement.
   (b) Dynamics: **sempre pianissimo.**

C. **Bartók's Comments.** Could be practised as a trill exercise. However, when played as intended, requires conspicuous finger control because it must be played softly. Not intended for the average pupil.

D. **Suggestions.** Begin practising at medium intensities. Be sure that all rests are observed and that syncopated notes are accented slightly.

No. 64. Line and Point.

A. **Technique.**

   1. TOUCH. **Legato** and **non-legato.**

   2. FINGER INDEPENDENCE. Part-playing in each hand.

   3. PEDALLING. Use of the damper.

B. **Musicianship.**

   1. NOTATION. Mixed accidentals.

   2. RHYTHM. 2/2.

   3. EXPRESSION.
     (a) Dynamics: **marcato.**

C. **Bartók's Comments.** 64a: From a sustained interval of a second, voices proceed in opposite directions. It is not considered difficult. Good illustration of bitonality and 2/2 meter. 64b: Chromatic figures proceeding from the same point an octave apart. Version "b" is a chromatic compression of version "a". This is the first example of compression from diatonic into chromatic.

D. **Suggestions.** Note the use of leger-line half and whole rests in M.12

and 16   respectively of no. 64a. Play Ex. 17.

No. 65. Dialogue.

A. **Technique.**

   1. TOUCH. **Staccato.**

   2. INTERVAL PLAYING. Fifths in each hand.

   3. ENSEMBLE PLAYING. Vocal accompaniment.

B. **Musicianship.**

   1. NOTATION. The vocal score.

   2. EXPRESSION.
     (a) Dynamics: >

C. **Bartók's Comments.** Song appearing in Book I (cf. no. 14) is here played with accompaniment. Suggestions for playing are in appendix: Referring to the notes in the preface the piece can be played without voice as follows: a) on one piano: the left hand plays the lower line of the accompaniment, the right hand plays the melody. In the last four bars the right hand continues to play the upper line of the accompaniment. b) on two pianos: one player plays the accompaniment in its original form, the other one plays the melody by doubling the upper octave. Exercises in different types of fifths would be of help. In *D* minor with altered sixth.

D. **Suggestions.** *D* Aeolian Mode.

If the piece is sung and self-accompanied, check for accuracy of pitch during the singing of the melody in M. 15 and 19.

" Ej - nye,   " Nem,
" Come, then,   " No!
" Bien, bien,   " Non

Play Ex. 18.

No. 66.   Melody Divided.

A. **Technique.**

1. TOUCH. **Legato** and **espressivo.**

2. HAND INDEPENDENCE.
   (a) Combined Touch-Forms: **legato** vs. **espressivo.**
   (b) Dynamic Contrasts: *p* vs. **più *p*.**
   (c) Accompanying Figurations: in each hand.

3. INTERVAL PLAYING.

4. EMBELLISHMENTS. Slow double-stop tremolos.

B. **Musicianship.**
    1. NOTATION. Change of clef in R.H. *D* key signature.
    2. EXPRESSION.
      (a) Dynamics.

    C. **Bartók's Comments.** Study in double notes in pentatonic melody, transposed. In *E* or mixed keys.

    D. **Suggestions.** Polytonal. This volume also dedicated to Peter Bartók. Prepare Ex. 19-20, Vol. III, and note that the meter signature indicates an additive rhythm consisting of units of $3 + 3 + 2$ eighth notes. Each unit should be accented as indicated by the solid and dotted bar lines (use of a metronome will be especially helpful).

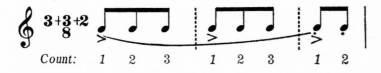

Play the exercise in 4/4 for the purpose of comparing the two types of rhythm. Note: 4/4 is a divisive rhythm.[4]

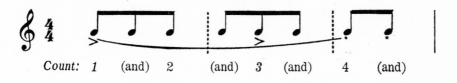

---

4 See No. 103 (D. Suggestions) for a more detailed explanation of divisive and additive rhythms.

Nos. 67-96

(Ex. 19-31)

No. 67.   Thirds Against a Single Voice.

A. **Technique.**

1. TOUCH. **Legato** and **non-legato.**
2. HAND INDEPENDENCE.
   (a) Counterpoint: as indicated in the title.
   (b) Dynamic Contrasts: > in R.H.
3. INTERVAL PLAYING. Thirds in each hand.

B. **Musicianship.**

1. RHYTHM. Syncopation.
2. EXPRESSION.
   (a) Dynamics: seven-bar **crescendo.**

C. **Bartók's Comments.** Nothing special to consider. Consult exercises in appendix.

D. **Suggestions.** Be sure that all tied notes are held for their full value and that there is evenness of articulation when playing the **legato** thirds in each hand. See **Suggestions** in no. 66, above.

No. 68.   Hungarian Dance.

A. **Technique.**

1. TOUCH. **Legato, staccato** and **tenuto.**
2. HAND INDEPENDENCE.
   (a) Counterpoint.
   (b) Combined Touch-Forms: **legato** vs. **staccato** and **tenuto, staccato** vs. **tenuto.**
3. INTERVAL PLAYING.
4. ACCOMPANYING FIGURATIONS. In each hand.
5. ENSEMBLE PLAYING. Two pianos, four hands.

B. **Musicianship.**

1. NOTATION. *D* key signature.
2. EXPRESSION.
   (a) Tempo: **con spirito** = with spirit.

C. **Bartók's Comments.** Can be played without the second piano part. A colorful piece for two pianos. Key of *D*.

D. **Suggestions.** If only one piano is available, the teacher or another pianist can play the upper staff of the **secondo** part an octave higher than written. Practise both parts. Prepare Ex. 21 which is the first example of **staccato** chord playing in the **Mikrokosmos.**

This piece is representative of the "new style" of Hungarian peasant music which, according to Bartók's estimate, began to develop about 140-160 years ago (the "old style" is over a thousand years old!). Characteristics are the eleven-syllable tune line (the first two measures contain eleven notes), use of the major scale rather than a pentatonic scale, the rounded (A A^5 B A) structure, and the possible use of the tune for singing as well as dancing.

No. 69.   Chord Study.

A. **Technique.**

1. TOUCH. **Staccato, tenuto** and **espressivo.**
2. HAND INDEPENDENCE.
   (a) Combined Touch-Forms: **staccato** and **tenuto** vs. **espressivo.**
   (b) Dynamic Contrast: *p* vs. *mf.*
   (c) Accompanying Figurations: in each hand.
3. CHORD PLAYING. Triads in each hand.
4. PASSAGE-WORK. Chordal, R.H. only.

B. **Musicianship.**

1. EXPRESSION.
   (a) Terms: **cantabile** = in a singing style (that is, with **espressivo** touch).

C. **Bartók's Comments.** See exercise in appendix. Simple basic triads good for hand position in grasping chords and playing crisp **staccato.** The accompaniment could be simplified as follows:

etc.

In bars 10-11,

14-15,

22-23,

26-27, 30,

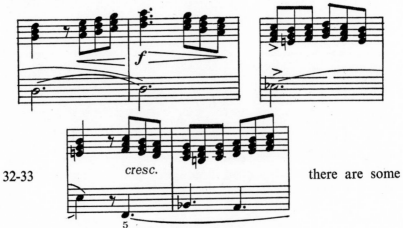

32-33   there are some

slight difficulties.

D. **Suggestions.** Bartók transcribed this piece for two pianos under the title, "Chord and Trill Study" (no. 2 in **Seven Pieces from "Mikrokosmos,"** published by Boosey and Hawkes). In this transcription, no. 69 appears as the **secondo** part in which the melody and some chords contain octave doublings. The transcription is suitable for performance by certain pianists and it may be used effectively as a recital piece in which the teacher or an advanced pianist plays the **primo** part. Béla and Ditta Bartók can be heard in the definitive performance of the transcription: see REMINGTON R19994.

No. 70. Melody Against Double Notes.

A. **Technique.**

1. TOUCH. **Legato** and **espressivo.**
2. HAND INDEPENDENCE.
    (a) Combined Touch-Form: **legato** vs. **espressivo.**
    (b) Dynamic Contrast: *p* vs. *f.*
    (c) Accompanying Figurations: in each hand.
3. INTERVAL PLAYING. In each hand.
4. POSITION. Crossed hands: R.H. over, L.H. under.

B. **Musicianship.**

1. NOTATION. *B* key signature in R.H., *C* key signature in L.H. Bass clef in each hand.
2. EXPRESSION.
    (a) Terms: **calando** = decreasing in intensity and speed.

C. **Bartók's Comments.** Polytonal.[1] R.H. is in *F♯* minor with raised sixth [*F♯* Dorian Mode]. The signature is actually *B* major but the piece is written in dominant [*F♯*] minor. L.H. is in *D* minor.

D. **Suggestions.** Practise first for mastery of touch and then work for control of dynamic contrast. Review Ex. 19-20 in preparation for no. 71.

No. 71. Thirds.

A. **Technique.**

1. TOUCH. **Legato** and **tenuto.**
2. HAND INDEPENDENCE.
    (a) Counterpoint in thirds.
3. FINGER INDEPENDENCE. Part-playing in L.H. only.

---

1 See explanation page 80.

B. **Musicianship.**

1. RHYTHM. Change of time: 2/2, 3/2.

2. EXPRESSION.
   (a) Tempo: **un poco più mosso** = a little faster. Tempo I
   = at the tempo indicated by the first tempo mark
   (M.M. = 66).

C. **Bartók's Comments.** Note changes of meter and tempo, also
F major R.H. vs. *D* minor L.H. Key of *D* minor ending on a major
triad. Dignified, quiet atmosphere. Note how theme comes to rest
on a major chord.

D. **Suggestions.** Begin Ex. 23a,b here in advance preparation for
no. 73. Practise hands separately at first, working for evenness of
finger articulation of the **legato** thirds.

No. 72.   Dragon's Dance.

A. **Technique.**

1. TOUCH. **Legato, non-legato, tenuto** and **staccato.**

2. HAND INDEPENDENCE.
   (a) Combined Touch-Form: **legato** vs. **tenuto** and **non-
   legato.**
   (b) Dynamic Contrast: **marcatissimo** vs. **tenuto.**

3. FINGER INDEPENDENCE. Part-playing in each hand.

B. **Musicianship.**

1. NOTATION. Change of clef in L.H. Mixed accidentals.

2. EXPRESSION.
   (a) Tempo: **Molto pesante** = very ponderously, heavily.

C. **Bartók's Comments.** Tonality and intervals lend a bizarre
effect. Pay attention to phrasing of second voice. Key may be *G* or
it may be called a hovering or uncertain tonality.

D. **Suggestions.** Begin by playing hands separately, then together, at slow tempi. Attend with care all **legato-staccato** markings.
Prepare Ex. 22, 23c,d.

No. 73.   Sixths and Triads.

A. **Technique.**

1. TOUCH. **Non-legato.**

2. HAND INDEPENDENCE.
   (a) Counterpoint.
3. INTERVAL AND CHORD PLAYING. As indicated by
   title.

B. **Musicianship.**
   1. EXPRESSION.
      (a) Dynamics: *f* **subito.**

C. **Bartók's Comments.** Again the major against minor in triads and their inversions. Key of *C* ending on dominant chord. Could be practised in various ways and speeds. Plagal ending.

D. **Suggestions.** Can be played in the style of Ex. 23a: play all eighth notes **staccato** and all quarter and half notes **tenuto,** M.M. ♩ = 96-144.

Plagal ending: a cadence in which the final Tonic (I) chord is preceded by a Subdominant (IV, II or VI) harmony.

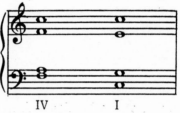

IV   I

In this piece, the Dominant replaces the Tonic as the final chord and it is preceded by what may be termed either the Subdominant seventh chord or a bimodal chord structure (vi + IV).

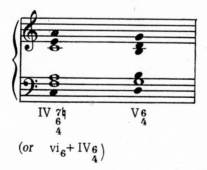

No. 74. Hungarian Song.

A. **Technique.**
   1. TOUCH. **Legato, non-legato** and **tenuto.**

   2. HAND INDEPENDENCE.
     (a) Combined Touch-Forms: **legato** vs. **non-legato** and **tenuto.**
     (b) Dynamic Contrasts: *mf* and *sf* vs. *f.*
     (c) Accompanying Figurations: in each hand.
   3. FINGER INDEPENDENCE. Part-playing in each hand.
   4. ENSEMBLE PLAYING. Accompanied song.

B. **Musicianship.**
   1. NOTATION. Reading of vocal score.
   2. RHYTHM. Syncopation.

   C. **Bartók's Comments.** Written first as a piano solo, then as song with accompaniment. Valuable for learning how to accompany. Pupil and/or teacher should sing the melody. See the relative notes in the preface.

   D. **Suggestions.** Observe the interruption of **legato** as indicated

by the separating sign in L.H., m. 32 of parts "a"

and "b."

The Hungarian title of this piece indicates it to be a teasing song to pair off a courting couple.

No. 75. Triplets.

   A. **Technique.**
   1. TOUCH. **Legato.**
   2. HAND INDEPENDENCE.
     (a) Counterpoint.
   3. FINGER INDEPENDENCE. Part-playing in each hand.
   4. BROKEN CHORD PLAYING. In each hand.

B. **Musicianship.**

    1. RHYTHM. Subdivision of the beat into two and three parts: the quarter note as the pulse unit in 2/4 and 3/4.

    2. EXPRESSION.

      (a) Tempo: **poco allarg.** = growing a little slower.

    C. **Bartók's Comments.** Interesting rhythmic patterns. Key of *D*. Notice change of meter and accents.

    D. **Suggestions.** It is recommended that Ex. 24 should be played here in preparation for no. 76 (the exercise seems to have little pertinency to no. 77).

No. 76. In Three Parts.

A. **Technique.**

    1. TOUCH. **Legato** and **staccatissimo.**

    2. HAND INDEPENDENCE.

      (a) Combined Touch-Forms: **legato** vs. **staccatissimo.**

      (b) Dynamic Contrast: ∧ vs. *f.*

    3. FINGER INDEPENDENCE. Part-playing in each hand.

B. **Musicianship.**

    1. NOTATION. Devised *G* key signature.

    2. RHYTHM. 2/2.

    3. EXPRESSION.

      (a) Tempo: **Allegro molto** = very fast.

      (b) Dynamics: **marcato** = marked, accented.

    C. **Bartók's Comments.** Note placement of the sharp in the key signature. Tied notes over moving voice require good finger control. Key of *G* ending on dominant chord.

    D. **Suggestions. Staccatissimo** is the most percussive touch-form employed by Bartók, who specifies that the sound is to be "almost sharp." The key should be released as quickly as possible after depression. Prepare Ex. 25.

No. 77. Little Study.

A. **Technique.**

    1. TOUCH. **Legato, staccato** and **tenuto.**

2. HAND INDEPENDENCE.
   (a) Counterpoint.
   (b) Combined Touch-Forms: **legato** vs. **staccato.**
3. BROKEN CHORD PLAYING. In each hand. Some intervals in L.H.
4. PASSAGE-WORK. Scalar passages in each hand.

B. **Musicianship.**
   1. NOTATION. *F* key signature.
   2. RHYTHM. Subdivision of the beat into four and six parts: the quarter note as the unit of pulse in 2/4 and 3/4.

C. **Bartók's Comments.** Good for finger facility and parallel direction. *G* minor, ending on *G* major chord. Good example in appendix.

D. **Suggestions.** In the last measure, the R.H. can be counted as follows:

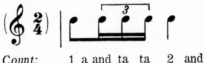

Count: 1 a and ta ta   2 and

No. 78.   Five-Tone Scale.

A. **Technique.**
   1. TOUCH. **Legato.**
   2. HAND INDEPENDENCE.
      (a) Counterpoint.
      (b) Dynamic Contrast: $>$ vs. f.
      (c) Accompanying Figurations: in R.H. only.
   3. BROKEN CHORD PLAYING. In each hand.
   4. EMBELLISHMENTS. Slow trill in R.H.

B. **Musicianship.**
   1. RHYTHM. Syncopation. **ben ritmato** $=$ rhythmically.
   2. EXPRESSION.
      (a) Dynamics.

C. **Bartók's Comments.** Voices are in five-note ranges in changing position. In *E* minor. Consonant chords.

D. Suggestions. Note the tied notes in the last two bars.

Play Ex. 26-28 and be sure the accents are observed in Ex. 27 and 28.

No. 79. Hommage à J.S.B.

A. **Technique.**
1. TOUCH. **Legato.**
2. HAND INDEPENDENCE.
  (a) Counterpoint.
  (b) Dynamic Contrast: > vs. *p*, *mp* and *mf.*
3. BROKEN CHORD PLAYING. In each hand.
4. EMBELLISHMENTS. Slow tremolo in each hand (m. 17).

B. **Musicianship.**
1. NOTATION. *G* key signature. Mixed accidentals. The sixteenth rest.
2. RHYTHM. Subdivision of the beat into four parts: the quarter note as the pulse unit in 3/4. The dotted eighth-sixteenth note rhythm. Syncopation.
3. EXPRESSION.
  (a) Tempo: **Calmo** = tranquilly, calmly.
    poco rit. = gradually a little slower.
    ritard. = growing slower.
    a tempo = return to the original tempo.

C. **Bartók's Comments.** Signature looks like *E* minor but the piece is written in *E* major. In no fixed key. Left hand imitates right hand figures in inversion. Minor intervals are superimposed over major ones. Requires well-balanced playing. See exercises: variety of intervals from a set note. Also irregular accents.

D. **Suggestions.** Check carefully the playing of m. 16.

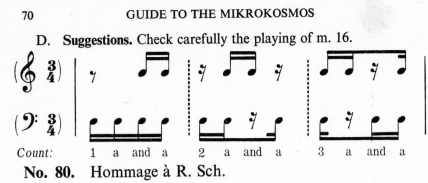

Count:　1　a　and　a　　2　a　and　a　　3　a　and　a

No. 80. Hommage à R. Sch.

A. **Technique.**

1. TOUCH. **Legato** and **staccatissimo.**

2. HAND INDEPENDENCE.
   (a) Counterpoint.
   (b) Dynamic Contrast: **in relievo.**
   (c) Combined Touch-Forms: **legato** vs. **staccatissimo.**
   (d) Accompanying Figurations: in each hand.

B. **Musicianship.**

1. NOTATION. *E♭* key signature. Mixed accidentals.

2. RHYTHM. The dotted eighth-sixteenth note rhythm.

3. EXPRESSION.
   (a) Tempo: **Andantino, piacevole** = faster than **andante,**
   played in a smooth non-accented manner.

C. **Bartók's Comments.** Employs the more complex and richer harmonies of the early Romantic Period. Atmosphere like Schumann's music.

D. **Suggestions.** There may be a tendency to play M. 17-20 (particularly M. 17 and 18) as dotted rhythms throughout.

Referring to Bartók's comments above, note in this piece the chromaticism, mellifluous parallel sixths, and diminished chords, all popular with certain Romantic (19th Century) composers.

No. 81.   Wandering.

A. **Technique.**

   1. TOUCH. **Legato.**

   2. HAND INDEPENDENCE.
     (a) Counterpoint.
     (b) Dynamic Contrast: *mp* vs. *p.*

B. **Musicianship.**

   1. NOTATION. Change of clef in L.H.

   2. RHYTHM. Change of time: 2/4, 3/4.

   3. EXPRESSION.
     (a) Tempo: **Non troppo lento** = not too slow.
     (b) Dynamics.

C. **Bartók's Comments.** Melodic figures repeated a tone higher or lower. Contrasting major and minor thirds. No fixed key. Abstract music.

D. **Suggestions.** Abstract music = Absolute music = music representative of nothing but musical ideas. In contradistinction to this is Program music with which is associated non-musical ideas such as a story or a picture. Program music almost always bears a descriptive title. In this piece, in view of Bartók's comment above, the title "Wandering" apparently refers to the meandering of the motive through the keys as if in search of a tonality. In actuality, a kind of "Bartókian neutral tonality" is achieved through (a) use of a major pentachord imitated in stretto[1] by a parallel minor pentachord in M. 1-14 and, (b) use of the same contrapuntal device, this time in inversion, whose bitonal materials consist of major pentachords a perfect fifth apart in M. 15ff. Prepare Ex. 29 (see **Bartók's Comments**) in no. 82 below).

No. 82.   Scherzo.

A. **Technique.**

   1. TOUCH. **Legato, non-legato, staccato and tenuto.**

---

[1] Stretto = a fugal device in which a musical idea (such as the pentachord illustrated above) is imitated or overlapped by the entry of another musical idea prior to the conclusion of the first idea.

2. HAND INDEPENDENCE.
   (a) Counterpoint.
   (b) Combined Touch-Forms: **tenuto** vs. **staccato.**
   (c) Dynamic Contrast: < vs. *mf.*

3. INTERVAL PLAYING. In each hand.

B. **Musicianship.**

1. NOTATION. *G* key signature.

2. RHYTHM. Change of time: 7/8, 3/8, 3/4, 2/4. Syncopation.

3. EXPRESSION.
   (a) Tempo: **Allegretto scherzando** == slower than allegro and in a playful, joking manner.
   (b) Dynamics: accents.

C. **Bartók's Comments.** Should be played crisply with *strong* accents, especially left hand. Appendix exercise demonstrates accented beats in 7/8 time.

D. **Suggestions.** Accent B. 1 and 5 in the first four bars.

Count: 1 2 3 4 5 6 7

Scherzo == joke, jest. This title can be given to an instrumental piece of a humorous character, whose leading features are animated movement, accentuation, and contrast.

No. 83.   Melody with Interruptions.

A. **Technique.**

1. TOUCH. **Legato, non-legato** and **tenuto.**

2. INTERVAL AND CHORD PLAYING. In each hand.

3. EMBELLISHMENTS. Slow double-stop tremolos in each hand.

4. PEDALLING. Use of the damper.

B. **Musicianship.**

1. EXPRESSION.
   (a) Dynamics: **marcato.**

C. **Bartók's Comments.** Hungarian folk tune: genuine, not made up. Double notes in trill form with repeated, strongly-accented notes which interrupt. Similar to theme in [Stravinsky's] **Petrouchka.**

D. **Suggestions.** Observe the syncopated pedalling. Every *g* in the R.H. is natural.

No. 84. Merriment.

A. **Technique.**
1. TOUCH. **Legato, non-legato, tenuto** and **espressivo (dolce).**
2. HAND INDEPENDENCE.
    (a) Counterpoint.
3. FINGERING INDEPENDENCE. Part-playing in each hand.
4. CHORD PLAYING. In R.H. only.
5. PEDALLING. Use of the damper.

B. **Musicianship.**
1. NOTATION. *A* key signature. Treble clef in each hand.
2. RHYTHM. Syncopation.
3. EXPRESSION.
    (a) Tempo: **tranquillo** = slower.
    (b) Dynamics: accents.

C. **Bartók's Comments.** Good study in syncopated rhythm. In Mixolydian Mode in *E* with minor seventh.

D. **Suggestions.** Take notice of the part-writing in M. 7 (R.H.) and 11 (L.H.).

Prepare Ex. 30-31. In m. 15 (b.3), place the first finger of each hand

on *a*.

No. 85.   Broken Chords.

    A. **Technique.**

        1. TOUCH. **Legato** and **tenuto.**

        2. FINGER INDEPENDENCE. Part-playing in R.H.

        3. BROKEN CHORD PLAYING. In each hand.

        4. POSITION. Hand crossings: R.H. under (**sotto**), L.H. over (**sopra**).

    B. **Musicianship.**

        1. NOTATION. Change of clef in L.H.

        2. RHYTHM. The eighth note duplet in 6/8.

        3. EXPRESSION.

            (a) Tempo: change of tempo.

            (b) Dynamics: accents, 8-bar **crescendo.**

    C. **Bartók's Comments.** Broken chord pattern in continuation from right hand to left hand and vice versa. Note the changes in rhythmic patterns. **Scorrevole** means fluently. Key is not very certain but it seems to be in *G*. Appendix exercises are based on all chords of the scale, with the seventh added, and their resolution. Very good to introduce here.

    D. **Suggestions.** M. 3, 27, and 59-60 can be counted *one-two-and three, four-five-and-six.* The second note of each duplet should be played on '**and.**'

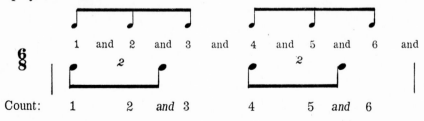

No. 86.   Two Major Pentachords.

A. **Technique.**
1. TOUCH. **Legato.**
2. HAND INDEPENDENCE.
   (a) Counterpoint.
   (b) Dynamic Contrast: *sf* vs. *p* **(crescendo).**
3. FINGER INDEPENDENCE. Part-playing in each hand.

B. **Musicianship.**
1. NOTATION. Reading of sharps in L.H. only.
2. RHYTHM. Syncopation.
3. EXPRESSION.
   (a) Tempo: change of tempo.
   (b) Dynamics: from *pp* to *ff*.

C. **Bartók's Comments.** Pentachord means the first five degrees of a scale of seven degrees. One voice in *C*, the other in *F♯* in juxtaposition. Often employed in modern music and when understood would solve many of its mysteries. Not for average pupils.

D. **Suggestions.** The first phrase begins in the L.H. and proceeds from bass to treble clef in the first four measures. The second phrase (M. 5-8) begins with the retrograde form[2] of m. 1.

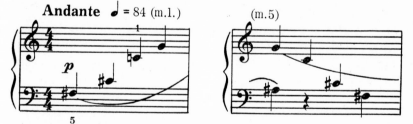

Note the half-note tie in the L.H. of the last two measures.

No. 87.   Variations.

A. **Technique.**
1. TOUCH. **Legato, tenuto,** dotted **tenuto** and **espressivo (cantabile, dolce).**
2. HAND INDEPENDENCE.
   (a) Combined Touch-Forms: **legato** vs. dotted **tenuto.**
   (b) Dynamic Contrasts: ∧ and *sf* vs. *f, p* vs. *pp*.

---

2 Crab motion or cancrizans (that is, the repetition of a musical idea in reverse order so that the last note begins and the first note ends the repetition).

3. FINGER INDEPENDENCE. Part-playing in each hand.

4. INTERVAL AND CHORD PLAYING. In each hand.

5. POSITION. Hand crossings: R.H. over.

B. Musicianship.

1. NOTATION. Clef changes in each hand.

2. RHYTHM. Change of time. Syncopation.

3. EXPRESSION.
   (a) Tempo: **Lo stesso tempo** = the same tempo.
   (b) Dynamics: accented voice parts, M. 34 and 36!

   (c) Phrasing: theme and two variations.

C. Bartók's Comments. Use of more involved chords against melody in right hand and then reversed to left hand. Note changes in tempos and rhythms. In *D* minor feeling but ending on 6/4 chord of *D* major.

D. Suggestions. Dotted **tenuto** is an agogic variation of **tenuto** touch: the key is pressed rather than struck down and the tone is sounded "usually for half the value of the note, never less." **Cantabile** and **dolce** are to be played with **espressivo** touch; in fact, the difference between them is one of dynamics (as indicated in the score).[3] A 6/4 chord is a triad or chord in the position of the second inversion.

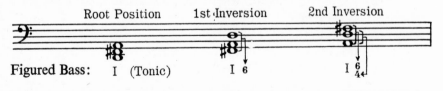

3 See also p. 14 for a complete explanation of touch-forms.

No. 88. Duet for Pipes.

A. Technique.

    1. TOUCH. **Espressivo (cantabile)** and **staccato.**

    2. HAND INDEPENDENCE.

       (a) Counterpoint.

    3. FINGER INDEPENDENCE. Last bar only.

    4. EMBELLISHMENTS. Slow trills in each hand.

B. Musicianship.

    1. NOTATION. The double flat. Treble clef in each hand.

    2. RHYTHM. Subdivision of the beat into two and three parts: the quarter note as the pulse unit in 2/4.

    3. EXPRESSION.

       (a) Tempo: change of tempo.

       (b) Phrasing: the separating sign.

    C. Bartók's Comments. Two pipes or flutes play chromatic melodies with skips and in triplets with various combinations.

    D. Suggestions. Play m. 4 **non-legato.**

Take notice of the interruption of **legato** between M. 22 and

23.   The accented, **staccato** sixteenth notes in the

last measure require almost the equivalent of **staccatissimo** touch.

Bartók's preliminary title, "Triplets," indicates the fundamental purpose of this piece.

No. 89.   In Four Parts.

A. **Technique.**

   1. TOUCH. **Legato, non-legato** and **tenuto.**

   2. FINGER INDEPENDENCE. Part-playing in each hand.

B. **Musicianship.**

   1. NOTATION. Devised two-sharp key signature.

   2. EXPRESSION.

     (a) Tempo: change of tempo.

     (b) Phrasing: separating signs.

C. **Bartók's Comments.** Four voices: sometimes in chord form, sometimes in contrapuntal style. Preclassical.

D. **Suggestions.** Observe the **non-legato** and the separating signs in the last two measures.

No. 90.   In Russian Style.

A. **Technique.**

   1. TOUCH. **Legato.**

   2. FINGER INDEPENDENCE. Part-playing in each hand.

   3. INTERVAL PLAYING. As accompanying figurations in each hand (minor seconds, major sevenths).

B. **Musicianship.**

   1. NOTATION. Change of clef in L.H. Mixed accidentals.

   2. RHYTHM. Subdivision of the beat into two and four parts: the half note as the pulse unit in 2/2.

   3. EXPRESSION.

     (a) Dynamics: **marcato e pesante.**

     (b) Phrasing: separating signs.

     (c) Terms: **Ossia** = alternative passage.

C. **Bartók's Comments.** Voice in left hand against a minor second in right hand resolved to a minor third. Major third resolved to an augmented fourth. Not an original Russian tune but in the style: short themes and sentences, repetition. Good time for explanation of augmented and diminished intervals in Key of *C*, etc.

D. **Suggestions.** Referring to the last four measures, L.H., compare the intervals with their inversions in the **Ossia:** major seventh-minor second, major sixth-minor third, perfect fifth-perfect fourth, and diminished fifth-augmented fourth.

Inverting an augmented fourth results in a diminished fifth and vice versa. Play these examples:

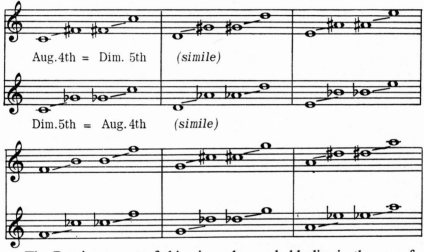

The Russian aspect of this piece also probably lies in the use of the tonal components [music notation] . Other more specific characteristics might be the use of duple meter, recurring rhythmic motives comprised of equal notes (quarter notes), and a kind of rhythmic solemnity arising from the use of short slurs which appear on each strong beat of the measure.

No. 91.   Chromatic Invention 1.

A. **Technique.**
   1. TOUCH. **Espressivo.**
   2. HAND INDEPENDENCE.
      (a) Counterpoint.
   3. FINGERING PROBLEMS. Chromatics.

B. **Musicianship.**
   1. NOTATION. Mixed accidentals. Clef change in L.H.
   2. EXPRESSION.
      (a) Dynamics: **smorzando** = fading away.

C. **Bartók's Comments.** Patterned after the form of Bach,
written in the chromatic idiom. Two-voice inventions, simple and
clear. Voices in direct imitation and inversion. Teaching of it can
be delayed if pupil is not ready.

D. **Suggestions.** Introduction (or review) of the chromatic scale
can be undertaken with this piece. Play this example one, two, three
and four to the beat for one, two, three and four octaves respectively,
increasing the indicated tempo slowly to M.M. ♩ = 120:

No. 92.   Chromatic Invention 2.

A. **Technique.**
   1. TOUCH. **Legato** and **non-legato.**
   2. HAND INDEPENDENCE.
      (a) Counterpoint.
      (b) Combined Touch-Forms: **legato** vs. **non-legato.**
      (c) Dynamic Contrasts: ∧ and *f* vs. *mf, f* vs. *ff.*
      (d) Accompanying Figurations: in each hand.
   3. POSITION. Hand crossings: R.H. over. Unison playing
      with the hands two and five octaves apart. One and
      two-octave leaps with the R.H. within a four-octave
      range.
   3. EMBELLISHMENTS. Slow trills in each hand.
   4. FINGERING PROBLEMS. Chromatics.

B. **Musicianship.**
   1. NOTATION. Clef changes in R.H. Leger-line notes in
      L.H. The sign *8*----------.
   2. RHYTHM. Syncopation.
   3. EXPRESSION.
      (a) Tempo: **Allegro robusto** = fast, firm and bold.

C. **Bartók's Comments.** Voices begin in unison. More freely written than the first invention and has entirely different character and spirit. Written within the limits of a pentachord with chromatic tones.

D. **Suggestions.** In m. 14, b. 1, the *a* remains sharp.

No. 93. In Four Parts.

A. **Technique.**

1. TOUCH. **Legato.**

2. FINGER INDEPENDENCE. Part-playing in each hand.

B. **Musicianship.**

1. NOTATION. *G* key signature (devised).

2. RHYTHM. Change of time: 2/4, 3/4, 5/8.

3. EXPRESSION.
(a) Phrasing: separating signs.
(b) Terms: **sonoro** = with a sonorous, ringing tone.

C. **Bartók's Comments.** Well-knit, four-voice study with an interesting and consistent rhythmic pattern. Note changes in meter. Key of *G*.

D. **Suggestions.** The **legato** should be interrupted between M. 10 and 11 (be careful not to interpolate an eighth rest here!).

In M. 13-14, the tied, dotted half notes in each hand must be held down.

No. 94. Tale.

  A. **Technique.**

      1. TOUCH. **Espressivo, tenuto** and dotted **tenuto.**

      2. HAND INDEPENDENCE.

        (a) Counterpoint.

      3. FINGER INDEPENDENCE. Part-playing in each hand.

  B. **Musicianship.**

      1. NOTATION. $E\flat$ key signature. Clef changes in each hand. Mixed accidentals.

      2. RHYTHM. Change of time.

      3. EXPRESSION.

        (a) Dynamics.

        (b) Phrasing: the comma (m. 10).

  C. **Bartók's Comments.** Descriptive little piece in contrapuntal form, alternating between 2/4 and 3/4 meters. Some polytonality. Key of *C* minor. Form is definite and very expressive.

  D. **Suggestions.** The comma (m. 10) is a separating sign which means "a slight, almost unnoticeable pause in which the time of separation is taken equally from the notes preceding and following the comma".

The Hungarian title can be interpreted as "Once upon a time . . ." See BR 1:6:1.

No. 95. Song of the Fox.

A. **Technique.**

   1. TOUCH. **Legato, non-legato, staccato, tenuto** and **portamento (portato).**

   2. HAND INDEPENDENCE.
      (a) Counterpoint.
      (b) Combined Touch-Forms: **legato** vs. **non-legato** and **portamento, non-legato** vs. **staccato** and **portamento,** and **tenuto** vs. **portamento.**

   3. FINGER INDEPENDENCE. Part-playing in L.H. only.

   4. INTERVAL AND CHORD PLAYING. In each hand.

   5. ENSEMBLE PLAYING. Vocal accompaniment.

B. **Musicianship.**

   1. NOTATION. The vocal score. *D* key signature. Change of clef (R.H., part "b").

   2. RHYTHM. Syncopation.

   3. EXPRESSION.
      (a) Phrasing: the separating signs | and '.
      (b) Terms: **poco a poco più tranquillo e rallentando al** = little by little growing quieter and slower until. **Ca.** = about.

C. **Bartók's Comments.** Good study in syncopated rhythm. Simple melody made interesting by variety in harmony and changes in tempo. When in song form, the accompaniment is simple but interestingly done. See the relative notes in the preface.

D. **Suggestions. Portamento (portato)** is a detached touch which combines key pressure (**tenuto** touch) with hand-motion (flexible wrist action) so that "the tone receives one-half the value of the note and is played without weight." Take notice of the separating signs

in M. 4, 8,  and 15 (comma!) of

part "a"

and M. 10 and 17

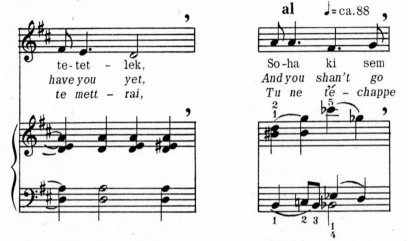

of part "b". This piece can be played as a self-accompanied vocal solo, a two-piano transcription, and/or an instrumental or vocal solo with piano accompaniment.

No. 96.   Stumblings.

A. **Technique.**

1. TOUCH. **Espressivo** and **staccato.**

2. HAND INDEPENDENCE.
   (a) Counterpoint.

3. BROKEN CHORD PLAYING. In each hand.

4. FINGERING PROBLEMS.

B. **Musicianship.**

1. NOTATION. *G* key signature. Leger-line notes above the staff in the bass clef.

2. EXPRESSION.
   (a) Dynamics.

C. **Bartók's Comments.** Good study for finger work in parallel motion. Good material for stressing arm co-ordination combined with fingers. Key of *G*.

D. **Suggestions.** The arrangement of the notes in M. 1-2 is suggestive of 6/8 time and, therefore, the pupil should be cautioned against interpolating accents anywhere except the first beat of a measure.

No. 97. Notturno.

A. **Technique.**
1. TOUCH. **Legato, staccato** and **espressivo.**
2. HAND INDEPENDENCE.
   (a) Combined Touch-Forms: **legato** vs. **espressivo** and **staccato.**
   (b) Accompanying Figurations: in each hand.
3. BROKEN CHORD PLAYING. In each hand.
4. PEDALLING. Use of the damper.

B. **Musicianship.**
1. NOTATION. *G* key signature.
2. RHYTHM. Subdivision of the beat into six parts: the dotted quarter as the pulse unit in 6/8. Polyrhythm (cross-rhythm): two (L.H.) vs. three (R.H.), m. 35.
3. EXPRESSION.
   (a) Phrasing: in ternary form.

C. **Bartók's Comments.** Nostalgic piece in *E* minor reminiscent of Chopin or Scriabin. Note left hand theme at end of piece.

D. **Suggestions.** Prepare Ex. 32, a study in passing of the thumb, as preparation for no. 98 and take notice of the **legato** vs. **staccato** and **marcato** accents in 7/8 time. As far as no. 97 is concerned, **Notturno** = nocturne = a piano piece of romantic or sentimental character usually lacking a distinct form. See BR 2:4:1.

No. 98. Thumb Under.

A. **Technique.**
1. TOUCH. **Legato.**
2. FINGERING PROBLEMS. Passing of the thumb.

B. **Musicianship.**
1. NOTATION. *F* key signature.
2. EXPRESSION.
   (a) Phrasing: separating signs.
   (b) Dynamics: accents.

C. **Bartók's Comments.** Not difficult but good for thumb crossing. Refer to exercise in appendix. In *F*, ending on the second tone.

D. **Suggestions.** Note interruption of **legato** between M.17 and

18.

No. 99. Crossed Hands.

A. **Technique.**

1. TOUCH. **Legato** and **tenuto.**
2. HAND INDEPENDENCE.
(a) Dynamic Contrasts: $>$, **p** and **f** vs. *mf.*
3. POSITION. Hand crossings: L.H. over.

B. **Musicianship.**

1. NOTATION. Devised one-flat (e♭) and two-sharp (f♯ and g♯) key signatures in R.H. and L.H. respectively. Clef changes in L.H.

C. **Bartók's Comments.** Difficult for some pupils because of different key signatures for each hand. Show combination of parts to make scale or diminished seventh chord. Key is uncertain.

D. **Suggestions.** According to Bartók's comment above, the parts can be combined to form the following scale and diminished chords.

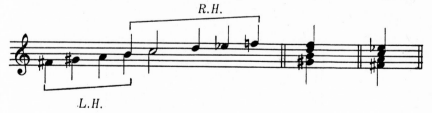

R.H.

L.H.

No. 100. In the Style of a Folk Song.

A. **Technique.**

1. TOUCH. **Espressivo.**
2. HAND INDEPENDENCE.
(a) Counterpoint.

B. **Musicianship.**
    1. RHYTHM. Subdivision of the beat into two parts: the eighth note as the pulse unit in 5/8. The dotted eighth —sixteenth note rhythm. Change of time: 5/8, 3/8.
    2. EXPRESSION.
        (a) Terms: **tutte le due voci con molta espressione** = both parts or voices with much expression.

C. **Bartók's Comments.** This resembles the Wagnerian "Magic Fire" theme from **Die Walküre.** Melody is long, written in two different positions. A Balkan melody, not my own invention.

D. **Suggestions.** Attend to the tied notes in the R.H. of the last two lines. See BR 1:3:1.

No. 101. Diminished Fifth.

A. **Technique.**
    1. TOUCH. **Legato.**
    2. HAND INDEPENDENCE.
        (a) Counterpoint.

B. **Musicianship.**
    1. EXPRESSION.
        (a) Tempo: **Con moto** = with animation.

C. **Bartók's Comments.** Two voices beginning at the interval of a diminished fifth and proceeding in various directions and patterns. Phrases are short and concise. Probably in the key of *D* minor, ending on diminished fifth.

D. **Suggestions.** Bitonal, based on the Aeolian tetrachord

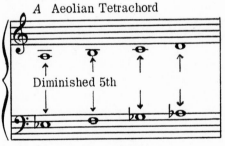

A Aeolian Tetrachord

Diminished 5th

E♭ Aeolian Tetrachord

transposed to various keys.[1] Juxtaposition of the hands may cause

---

1 Tetrachord = the first four degrees of a scale of seven degrees. In this case, the Aeolian Mode.

some difficulty at first. Be sure to observe the eighth rests in m. 5 in order to avoid collision of the hands when proceeding to m. 6.

No. 102. Harmonics.

A. **Technique.**

    1. TOUCH. **Legato, non-legato, staccato, staccatissimo tenuto, portamento** and **espressivo (dolce).**

    2. CHORD PLAYING. In each hand.

    3. POSITION. Hand crossing: R.H. over.

    4. EMBELLISHMENTS. Grace notes in R.H.

    5. PASSAGE-WORK. Scalar passages in R.H.

    6. PEDALLING. Use of the damper.

B. **Musicianship.**

    1. NOTATION. Use of diamond-shaped quarter, half, and dotted half notes. Use of treble clef in L.H. and clef change in R.H. The double sharp.

    2. RHYTHM. Subdivision of the beat into two, three, and four parts: the quarter note as the pulse unit. Change of time: 2/4, 3/4.

    3. EXPRESSION.

        (a) Tempo: **un poco rubato** = "robbed" a little in tempo. This direction means that the strict rhythmical flow can be modified by prolonging prominent melody notes or chords if there is an equivalent acceleration of less prominent tones. Changes of tempo.

        (b) Dynamics: *sff* = **sforzato.** This is the strongest accent sign used in the **Mikrokosmos.**

C. **Bartók's Comments.** Interesting effects produced from vibrations of overtones or harmonics when keys are silently pressed down and the same notes are sounded in a different range. Schoenberg was the first to use harmonics in three atonal pieces, Op. 11. Henry Cowell uses these and many other devices such as plucking the strings in various ways at long or short distances to produce unusual sound effects or colors.

D. **Suggestions.** This piece can be considered as a summary of technical and musical problems encountered heretofore in the **Mikrokosmos.** Concerning the playing of harmonics, slow key descent (use **tenuto** touch) will permit key depression without sounding of tones.

No. 103.   Minor and Major.

A. **Technique.**
1. TOUCH. **Legato, non-legato** and **espressivo.**
2. HAND INDEPENDENCE.
   (a) Counterpoint.
3. BROKEN CHORD PLAYING. In each hand.
4. POSITION. Hand crossings: R.H. over (L.H. under).

B. **Musicianship.**
1. NOTATION. Change of clef in R.H. Dotted bar lines.
2. RHYTHM. Change of time: 5/8, 6/8, 7/8, 8/8, 9/8, $\frac{3\times2}{8}$.

   9/8 as an additive $\frac{(4+5)}{8}$ rhythm and as a divisive (compound time) rhythm. The dotted bar lines in M. 5-6 indicate additive rhythms of $\frac{2+3+2}{8}$ and $\frac{3+2+3}{8}$. The sign $\frac{3\times2}{8}$ is another way of indicating 3/4 so that the eighth note continues to serve as the pulse unit. Note also that 5/8 is considered as $\frac{3+2}{8}$ and $\frac{2+3}{8}$.

3. EXPRESSION.
   (a) Tempo: Change of tempo. **Presto** $=$ faster than **allegro** and slower than **prestissimo. Accelerando** $=$ gradually growing faster.
   (b) Dynamics: *sff*, 15-bar **crescendo.**
   (c) Terms: **rep. ad libitum** $=$ the performer is free to repeat these measures (M. 37-38).

C. **Bartók's Comments.** This is a minor pentachord superimposed against a major in an interesting variety of meters. $\frac{3\times2}{8}$ instead of 3/4 so as not to change speed notes.

D. **Suggestions.** 9/8 meter is used here as a divisive (M. 19-24)
and as an additive (M. 1-4) rhythm. A divisive rhythm is one in
which the measure is divided into equal parts (in 9/8: four dotted
quarter notes). An additive rhythm, on the other hand, is one in
which the measure is composed of unequal groups added together
(in 9/8, a group of four plus a group of five eighth notes). The basic
difference between the two types of rhythm is one of accentuation.

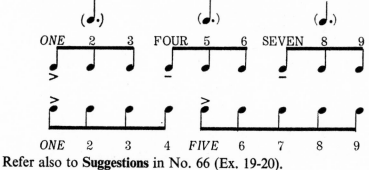

Refer also to **Suggestions** in No. 66 (Ex. 19-20).

No. 104. Through the Keys.

A. **Technique.**
  1. TOUCH. **Legato.**
  2. FINGERING PROBLEMS. Passing of the fingers.

B. **Musicianship.**
  1. NOTATION. *D, E♭, E, A,* and *B♭* key signatures. Change
     of clef in L.H.
  2. RHYTHM.

C. **Bartók's Comments.** Study in change of key without modul-
ation. Same theme in unison and in similar motion.

D. **Suggestions.** Also serves as a study in extension and contraction of the hands. Emphasize slightly the syncopated notes in
M. 14, 16, and 21.

(and in part "b").

The Hungarian title means "Wandering from one key to another."

No. 105.   Playing.

A. Technique.
1. TOUCH. **Legato, non-legato** and **tenuto.**
2. HAND INDEPENDENCE.
   (a) Counterpoint.
   (b) Dynamic Contrast: > vs. f.
3. FINGER INDEPENDENCE. Part-playing in each hand.
4. POSITION. Crossed hands: L.H. over, R.H. under.
5. FINGERING PROBLEMS. Black key playing in L.H. and white key playing in R.H.

B. Musicianship.
1. NOTATION. *E* key signature in L.H., *C* key signature in R.H. Treble clef in each hand.
2. RHYTHM. Change of time. Syncopation.
3. EXPRESSION.
   (a) Tempo: change of tempo.
   (b) Dynamics: **marcato.**

C. Bartók's Comments. Two pentatonic scales: a five-note scale

in *D* minor in the right hand and *C♯* minor in the left hand.

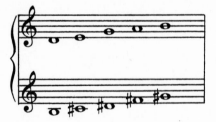

Similar to a theme in [Stravinsky's] **Sacre du Printemps.** Ends on dominant.

D. Suggestions. The separating signs in M. 12, 16 and 18

indicate phrase endings. Note the **marcato** (accents) in the alto

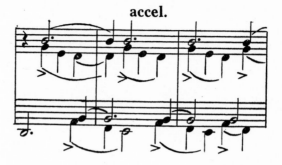

and bass voices of
M. 42-44.

No. 106. Children's Song.

A. **Technique.**
  1. TOUCH. **Legato.**
  2. HAND INDEPENDENCE.
     (a) Counterpoint.
     (b) Dynamic Contrasts: *p* vs. *mf* and *p*, **in rilievo.**
  3. FINGER INDEPENDENCE. Part-playing in L.H.

B. **Musicianship.**
  1. NOTATION. The tie sign between staves (M. 35-36).
     Change of clef in L.H.
  2. EXPRESSION.
     (a) Tempo: change of tempo.
     (b) Dynamics.

C. **Bartók's Comments.** A repetition of things done before.

D. **Suggestions.** Note the phrasing of M. 1-9 and the separating
sign in the L.H. of m. 26. Bring out the L.H.
slightly in M. 27-34.

No. 107.   Melody in the Mist.

A. **Technique.**
1. TOUCH. **Legato, non-legato** and **tenuto.**
2. CHORD PLAYING. In each hand.
3. POSITION. Interlocked hands.
4. PEDALLING. Use of the damper (or solo **sostenuto**) pedal.

B. **Musicianship.**
1. NOTATION. Mixed accidentals. **m.d.** $=$ right hand, **m.s.** $=$ left hand.
2. RHYTHM. Syncopation.

C. **Bartók's Comments.** Dissonant chords played a half-tone apart create a vague, misty impression. To understand range and tonality of chords, play them in continuity broken from left hand to right hand. The melody emerges from the mist to complete the phrase. This is built to a climax and disappears in the mist. Key of C.

D. **Suggestions.** Depress the damper pedal exactly as marked in the score. The pedal should be used also on b. 3 of M. 34 and 38 (release the damper on b. 1 of M. 35 and 39). Finger the chords in M. 41-44 as before. In M. 40-45, the pedal tones (*g* in each hand) can be sustained by depressing the middle or solo **sostenuto** (sustaining) pedal on b. 2 of m. 40, or by depressing the damper pedal as indicated. If the damper is used, replace the fingers silently on the pedal tones, b. 2 of

M. 44, and (keeping the keys held down) release the damper as marked in m. 45 (the last measure).

No. 108.   Wrestling.

A. **Technique.**
1. TOUCH. **Non-legato.**

2. FINGER INDEPENDENCE. Part-playing in each hand.

3. FINGERING PROBLEMS. Passing of the fingers.

B. **Musicianship.**

1. NOTATION. Mixed accidentals.

2. RHYTHM. Syncopation.

3. EXPRESSION.

(a) Dynamics: **sempre marcatissimo.** Always very marked or accented.

C. **Bartók's Comments.** Picturesque struggle between tones of a minor second. Both hands in unison. One voice is tied while the other continues within the small range of a pentachord with chromatic tones. There are superimposed major and minor thirds. The voices finally resolve to the major triad of *D.*

D. **Suggestions.** The final chord is "neutral" because of the simultaneous use of the major (*f♯*) and minor (*f♮*) third. The effect, however, is a kind of "hovering" major tonality. See BR 1:5:1.

No. 109.   From the Island of Bali.

A. **Technique.**

1. TOUCH. **Legato, non-legato, staccato, tenuto, espressivo (dolce)** and dotted **tenuto.**

2. HAND INDEPENDENCE.

(a) Counterpoint.

3. PEDALLING. Use of the solo **sostenuto** (sustaining) pedal, or the damper.

B. **Musicianship.**

1. NOTATION. Change of clef in L.H.

2. RHYTHM. Change of time: 6/8, 4/4.

3. EXPRESSION.

(a) Tempo: change of tempo.

(b) Phrasing: in ternary form.

(c) Terms: **(prol. Ped.)** = **pedale prolungato** = (optional) use of the solo **sostenuto** pedal.

C. **Bartók's Comments.** Impressionistic composition possibly describing a tropical scene. Then, some action or dance takes place in the **Risoluto** section, finally returning to the original tempo and mood. **Sostenuto** pedal could be used if you have one. Tonality uncertain but it ends on *D* minor and *F* minor.

D. Suggestions. If the piano is not equipped with a prolongation pedal, the half-depressed damper can be tried as a substitute (M. 30-38). See BR 1:2:2.

allarg.

(*prol.* ⅀ℰℬ.)

No. 110. Clashing Sounds.

A. **Technique.**

1. TOUCH. **Legato, non-legato,** and **tenuto.**
2. FINGER INDEPENDENCE. Part-playing in each hand.
3. INTERVAL PLAYING. In each hand.
4. POSITION. Interlocked hands.
5. PEDALLING. Use of the half-depressed damper.
6. EMBELLISHMENTS. Slow double-stop tremolos in each hand.

B. **Musicianship.**

1. NOTATION. Treble clef in each hand.
2. RHYTHM. Syncopation.
3. EXPRESSION.
   (a) Tempo: **Assai allegro** = very rapid, but not as fast as **molto allegro.** Tempo I, II.
   Un poco sostenuto = suddenly a little slower.
   (b) Dynamics: **mezza voce, ma marcato** = half-voice **(mezzo forte)** but marked or accented.
   (c) Terms: **come sopra** = as above (that is, **marcato**).

C. **Bartók's Comments.** Fifths in *C* and *D♭*, one against the other, beginning **mezza voce** with slower note values. The pattern is worked up to a frenzy of rhythmic sounds. This changes gradually to a **sostenuto** movement where the upper and lower voices of the chords proceed in unison. Tempo II returns, finally ending as it began with a common resolution to *f♭* and *e*. The pedal is held down for many measures, only it is put halfway down.

D. **Suggestions.** Bartók does not use the term **sostenuto** to indicate a gradual decrease in speed and, therefore, M. 21-29 should be played at M.M. = 140.

The Hungarian title means "And the tones sound and pound."

No. 111. Intermezzo.

A. **Technique.**

1. TOUCH. **Legato, tenuto** and **espressivo.**

2. HAND INDEPENDENCE.
   (a) Dynamic Contrasts: *p* vs. *mp*, *mf* vs. *mp.*
   (b) Combined Touch-Forms: **non-legato** vs. **legato** and **tenuto.**

3. FINGER INDEPENDENCE. Part-playing in each hand.

4. INTERVAL PLAYING. In the L.H. only.

5. PEDALLING. Use of the damper.

B. **Musicianship.**

1. NOTATION. *A* key signature. Mixed accidentals. Clef change in L.H.

2. RHYTHM. Change of time: 5/4, 3/4.

C. **Bartók's Comments.** Melody in melancholy mood in 3/4 and 5/4 in characteristic Hungarian style: it is a common device to repeat the melody a fifth higher. In *F♯* minor ending on the dominant.

D. **Suggestions.** The intervals in the L.H. of M. 48-49 are to be

played **non-legato**

and, in the same hand, *f* is natural in M. 38-40.

No. 112.   Variations on a Folk Tune.

    A. **Technique.**

       1. TOUCH. **Legato, non-legato** and **staccato.**

       2. HAND INDEPENDENCE.
         (a) Counterpoint.

       3. FINGER INDEPENDENCE. Part-playing in each hand.

       4. INTERVAL PLAYING. In each hand.

       5. PASSAGE-WORK. Scalar double sixths in each hand.

       6. FINGERING PROBLEMS.

    B. **Musicianship.**

       1. RHYTHM. Change of time.

       2. EXPRESSION.
         (a) Dynamics.

    C. **Bartók's Comments.** This is an original Hungarian song. Everybody knows this tune, even the Russians, Poles, and Slovaks. Theme is announced in single tones, repeated in double sixths, and then in four-voice form in slower tempo. Then the theme is repeated in sixths, **vivace.** Diatonic is compressed into chromatic tonality.

    D. **Suggestions.** Note fingering in the first lines and in m. 45. Observe **crescendo** marks. Prepare Ex. 33: here the L.H. brings out the additive rhythm of 4 + 3 and the R.H. plays **legato** and without accentuation (**leggero**).

No. 113.   Bulgarian Rhythm (1).

    A. **Technique.**

       1. TOUCH. **Legato** and **staccato.**

       2. HAND INDEPENDENCE.
         (a) Combined Touch-Forms: **legato** vs. **staccato.**
         (b) Dynamic Contrast: *mf* vs. *f* and *mp*, *mp* vs. *p.*
         (c) Accompanying Figurations: L.H. only.

       3. POSITION. Interlocked hands.

    B. **Musicianship.**

       1. RHYTHM. 7/8 meter. Syncopation.

2. EXPRESSION.

(a) Dynamics: **leggero** = lightly, without accentuation.

C. **Bartók's Comments.** The repetition can be played this way:  with octaves throughout. In this case, the "seconda volta" shall be played louder than the "prima volta." In order to develop the sense of rhythm it is recommended to play the piece as follows: two players (the exercise is useful even for more advanced players) who are able to play the piece perfectly shall play it as a piano duet, the second player playing the three introductory and the six closing bars and the accompaniment doubled in the lower octave (with both hands), the first player playing the melody doubled in the upper octave. Both parts should be studied by each.

The theme is Hungarian and the rhythm is Bulgarian. Bulgarian rhythm has short units. 7/8 meter. The melody is syncopated and not symmetrical. 7/8 and 5/8 time are very common in Bulgarian music. Metronome time means to play 49 measures in one minute (including the repetition).

D. **Suggestions.** Play the L.H. without accentuation (**leggero**).

See the two-piano transcription (no. 1) in **Seven Pieces from "Mikrokosmos."** See also BR 1:1:1.

No. 114. Theme and Inversion.

A. **Technique.**

1. TOUCH. **Legato** and **tenuto.**
2. HAND INDEPENDENCE.
   (a) Counterpoint.
   (b) Combined Touch-Forms: **legato** vs. **tenuto.**

B. **Musicianship.**

1. NOTATION. *D* key signature. Clef changes in each hand. Mixed accidentals.
2. RHYTHM. Change of time.
3. EXPRESSION.
   (a) Dynamics.

C. **Bartók's Comments.** Theme must be clearly outlined and presented to the pupil. Explain its arrangement. It is a combination of *B* minor and *E* minor.

D. **Suggestions.** The first two bars contain an introductory phrase which is repeated in varied form in M. 9-10, 17-18. The theme itself begins in m. 3 and is repeated in inverted form in m. 11.

See BR 2:5:3.

No. 115. Bulgarian Rhythm (2).

A. **Technique.**

1. TOUCH. **Legato.**

2. HAND INDEPENDENCE.
   (a) Counterpoint.

3. FINGER INDEPENDENCE. Part-playing in L.H.

4. INTERVAL AND BROKEN CHORD PLAYING. Minor sevenths in L.H. and arpeggios in each hand.

5. FINGERING PROBLEMS.

B. **Musicianship.**

1. NOTATION. Clef change in L.H. Mixed accidentals.

2. RHYTHM. 5/8 as $\frac{3+2}{8}$ and $\frac{2+3}{8}$.

3. EXPRESSION.
   (a) Phrasing: in ternary form.
   (b) Terms: **scorrevole** (fluently).

C. **Bartók's Comments.** This is an original Bulgarian theme. Altered key of *G*.

D. **Suggestions.** Check the hand-to-hand **legato** in M. 9-16 for steady dynamic level and clarity in articulation (there may be a tendency here to play **legatissimo**).

No. 116.   Melody.

A. **Technique.**
  1. TOUCH. **Legato, non-legato, staccato, tenuto,** dotted **tenuto, portamento** and **espressivo (cantabile).**
  2. HAND INDEPENDENCE.
     (a) Counterpoint.
     (b) Combined Touch-Forms: **legato** and **espressivo** vs. **tenuto,** dotted **tenuto** and **portamento.**
     (c) Dynamic Contrast: > vs. *p.*
  3. CHORD PLAYING. In each hand.
  4. PEDALLING. Use of the damper.
  5. PASSAGE-WORK. Scalar passages in each hand.

B. **Musicianship.**
  1. NOTATION. The double-dotted half note. Clef changes in each hand.
  2. EXPRESSION.
     (a) Tempo: **Tempo di Marcia** = march time. Change of tempo.
     (b) Dynamics.

C. **Bartók's Comments.** Same framework at introduction and at end. In Hungarian structure. Key of *G.*

D. **Suggestions.** A difficult piece in terms of variety of touch; in fact, all the non-percussive touch-forms are to be found here in various combinations. The second dot of a double-dotted note in turn adds half the value of the preceding dot to the note. See BR 2:1:2.

Hungarian structural characteristics include eleven-syllable phrases (M. 8-9, 10-11, 12-13, etc.); "punctuated" (syncopated) rhythms such as the eighth—dotted quarter pattern on the strong beat of M. 2, 15, etc.; **lassu** or slow section followed by a **friss** (M. 8ff.) or fast section; and the descending repetitions of the theme in M. 8-9.

No. 117.   Bourrée.

A. **Technique.**
  1. TOUCH. **Legato** and dotted **tenuto.**
  2. HAND INDEPENDENCE.
     (a) Counterpoint.
     (b) Combined Touch-Forms: **legato** vs. dotted **tenuto.**
     (c) Dynamic Contrasts: *sf* vs. *p,* > vs. *mf.*

3. BROKEN CHORD PLAYING. In the L.H.
4. POSITION. Hand crossing: R.H. over.
5. PASSAGE-WORK. Scalar passages in each hand.

B. **Musicianship.**
1. NOTATION. Clef changes in each hand. Mixed accidentals.
2. RHYTHM. Change of time: 4/4, 5/4, 3/2.
3. EXPRESSION.
   (a) Dynamics.

C. **Bartók's Comments.** Name of piece derived from the rhythm, similar to Couperin.

D. **Suggestions.** Bourrée = an old dance of French or Spanish origin. The tempo does not change in M. 23 and 26 since the quarter note remains the unit of pulse.

No. 118.   Triplets in 9/8 Time.

A. **Technique.**
1. TOUCH. **Legato.**
2. HAND INDEPENDENCE.
   (a) Counterpoint.
   (b) Dynamic Contrast: > vs. *p* and *mf.*
3. PASSAGE-WORK. Scalar passages in each hand.

B. **Musicianship.**
1. NOTATION. Clef changes in R.H.
2. RHYTHM. 9/8 as a compound triple meter.
3. EXPRESSION.
   (a) Dynamics: accents.

C. **Bartók's Comments.** None.

D. **Suggestions.** A study also in accentuation. Review explanation of accent marks on p. 24. See BR 2:4:2.

No. 119. Dance in 3/4 Time.

A. **Technique.**

    1. TOUCH. **Legato, staccato** and **tenuto.**

    2. HAND INDEPENDENCE.
        (a) Counterpoint.
        (b) Combined Touch-Forms: **legato** vs. **staccato.**

    3. POSITION. Hand crossing: L.H. under.

    4. PEDALLING. Use of the damper.

    5. PASSAGE-WORK. Scalar passages in each hand.

    6. FINGERING PROBLEMS.

B. **Musicianship.**

    1. NOTATION. *E* key signature.

    2. EXPRESSION.
        (a) Tempo: **Allegretto grazioso** = moderately fast and gracefully. **Pochiss. allarg.** = "a very little" gradual decrease in speed.
        (b) Dynamics.

C. **Bartók's Comments.** Key of *E* — kind of a Mixolydian tonality.

D. **Suggestions.** Note the **fermata** between M. 27-28. Pause here slightly (one or two beats).

No. 120. Fifth Chords.

A. **Technique.**

    1. TOUCH. **Legato, non-legato, staccato** and **tenuto.**

    2. FINGER INDEPENDENCE. Part-playing in each hand.

    3. CHORD PLAYING. Triads in each hand.

    4. POSITION. Interlocked hands.

B. **Musicianship.**

1. NOTATION. Change of clef in each hand.

2. RHYTHM. Change of time: 5/4, 3/2, 4/4, 3/4.

3. EXPRESSION.
(a) Tempo: **accelerando** from M.M. $\downarrow = 160$ to $\downarrow = 108$.
(b) Dynamics.

C. **Bartók's Comments.** Device of blocked small chords. Altered *C* major. Has great technical value. Must be played with a very pointed touch and accentuation.

D. **Suggestions.**
In *C* Mixolydian Mode.
See BR 1:2:1.

No. 121.   Two-Part Study.

A. **Technique.**

1. TOUCH. **Legato** and **non-legato.**

2. HAND INDEPENDENCE.
(a) Counterpoint.
(b) Combined Touch-Forms: **legato** vs. **non-legato.**

3. PASSAGE-WORK. Scalar passages in each hand.

4. FINGERING PROBLEMS.

B. **Musicianship.**

1. NOTATION. *A* key signature. Mixed accidentals.

2. RHYTHM. Change of time: 3/2, 4/4, 5/4, 3/4, 6/4. Syncopation.

C. **Bartók's Comments.** Different tonalities and scales. Mixed major and minor. Unusual procedure at end of piece.

D. Suggestions. Note separating signs which indicate interruption of **legato** in L.H. of M. 15 and 16.

Be sure to observe the R.H. tie in the last two measures so that the leading tone ($c\sharp$ in L.H.) resolves properly to the tonic (d in R.H.).

No. 122.   Chords Together and Opposed.

A. **Technique.**

   1. TOUCH. **Non-legato** and **tenuto.**

   2. HAND INDEPENDENCE.
   (a) Counterpoint.
   (b) Combined Touch-Forms: **legato** vs. **tenuto.**
   (c) Dynamic Contrast: ∧ vs. *f*.

   3. INTERVAL AND CHORD PLAYING. In each hand.

   4. PEDALLING. Use of the damper.

B. **Musicianship.**

   1. NOTATION. Clef changes in each hand. *G* key signature.

   2. RHYTHM. Syncopation.

   3. EXPRESSION.
   (a) Dynamics: accents.

C. **Bartók's Comments.** Key of *G*. Tonic and dominant chords superimposed or against each other. Chords have foreign tones or they could be called eleventh or thirteenth chords. Framework of the chord is often the same with inner voices moving up or down the scale. Ends on chords of *G* and *C* with consecutive fifths added to each. Good for strengthening fingers in inner voices and for fast repetition. Foreign tones add color.

D. **Suggestions.** Note the key change in m. 49

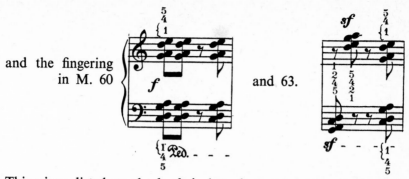

and the fingering in M. 60 and 63.

This piece, listed on the back jacket, does not appear in Bartók's recording (Columbia ML4419) of the **Mikrokosmos.**

No. 123. Staccato and Legato.

A. **Technique.**

1. TOUCH. **Staccato, legato** and **tenuto.**

2. HAND INDEPENDENCE.
    (a) Counterpoint.
    (b) Combined Touch-Forms: **legato** vs. **staccato** and **tenuto.**

B. **Musicianship.**

1. NOTATION. Mixed accidentals.

2. EXPRESSION.
    (a) Phrasing: canon at the fifth (part "b") and lower fifth (part "a").

C. **Bartók's Comments.** Key of *C* with much chromaticism. Requires keen observation and good control of fingers to make quick changes in touch.

D. **Suggestions.** Bartók's original title for this piece was "Staccato versus Legato."

A transcription of this piece appears in **Seven Pieces from "Mikrokosmos"** and it is recommended that the pianist should play the **primo** and **secondo** parts with the teacher or another performer.

No. 124.   Staccato.

A.   **Technique.**

1. TOUCH. **Staccato.**

2. HAND INDEPENDENCE.
   (a) Counterpoint.
   (b) Dynamic Contrasts: *sf* and *f* vs. *p.*

3. FINGERING PROBLEMS.

B.   **Musicianship.**

1. NOTATION. Mixed accidentals. Changes of clef in R.H.

2. EXPRESSION.
   (a) Tempo: **Allegretto mosso** = rapidly but not as fast as
       allegro.
   (b) Dynamics.
   (c) Terms: **secco quasi pizz.** = dry as if plucked.

C.   **Bartók's Comments.** Repeated notes in crisp, rapid **staccato**
touch. Requires light, fast movements, strong accentuations, and
variety of shading. Can be very effective if played with vitality.

D.   **Suggestions.** To be played with percussive finger-stroke. The
sforzato accents can be considered as designations of **staccatissimo**
touch.

No. 125.   Boating.

A.   **Technique.**

1. TOUCH. **Legato, staccato** and **espressivo (cantabile).**

2. HAND INDEPENDENCE.
   (a) Combined Touch-Forms: **legato** vs. **staccato** and
       espressivo.
   (b) Dynamic Contrast: *p* vs. *mf* and **più *p.***
   (c) Accompanying Figurations: in each hand.

3. BROKEN CHORD PLAYING. In each hand.

4. POSITION. Hand crossing: L.H. over.

B.   **Musicianship.**

1. NOTATION. Clef changes in L.H.

2. RHYTHM. Change of time.

3. EXPRESSION.
   (a) Tempo: **pochett. rit.** = "a very little" **ritardando.**
   (b) Phrasing: in ternary form.

C. **Bartók's Comments.** Descriptive piece in a very unusual tonality. Repetition gives feeling of monotonous motion of the water.

D. **Suggestions.** In m. 46 the R.H. replaces the L.H. *b* natural

on the third beat. See BR 2:5:2.

No. 126. Change of Time.

A. **Technique.**

1. TOUCH. **Non-legato.**
2. INTERVAL AND CHORD PLAYING. In each hand.
3. PEDALLING. Use of the damper.

B. **Musicianship.**

1. NOTATION. *F* key signature.
2. RHYTHM. Change of time: 2/4, 3/4, 3/8, 5/8, 6/8.

C. **Bartók's Comments.** Unusual changes of time and construction. This is similar to Rumanian style. The phrase structure is made up of one measure each of 2/4, 3/4, 3/8, and 5/8. This is consistently followed through more than one-half of the composition. The signature looks like *F* but the piece ends on the dominant of *C*. Count with the eighth note as the unit.

D. **Suggestions.** The syncopation pattern formed by the phrase structure should be counted with the eighth note as the unit of measurement:

$$\frac{2}{4} \left(\frac{4}{8}\right) \quad \frac{3}{4} \left(\frac{6}{8}\right) \quad \frac{3}{8} \quad \frac{5}{8}$$

Count: 1 2 3 4   1 2 3 4 5 6   1 2 3   1 2 3 4 5

See BR 2:1:1.

No. 127. New Hungarian Folk Song.

A. Technique.

1. TOUCH. **Legato, non-legato, staccato, tenuto,** dotted **tenuto** and **portamento.**
2. HAND INDEPENDENCE.
   (a) Combined Touch-Forms: **legato** vs. **staccato, tenuto** and dotted **tenuto.**
3. FINGER INDEPENDENCE. Part-playing in R.H.
4. INTERVAL PLAYING. Broken octaves in L.H.
5. CHORD PLAYING. In each hand.
6. EMBELLISHMENTS. Five-note turn in L.H.
7. ENSEMBLE PLAYING. Vocal accompaniment.

B. Musicianship.

1. NOTATION. *D* key signature. Clef changes in each hand.
2. RHYTHM. Change of time. Syncopation.
3. EXPRESSION.
   (a) Tempo: **pochiss. allarg.** = "a very little" gradual decrease in speed.

C. **Bartók's Comments.** This piece can be performed as follows: a) the same performer singing and accompanying himself; b) on two pianos, the first player playing the melody by doubling the octave, the second player by playing the original accompaniment; c) for violin and piano. The violinist plays the first verse in the original position, the second in the higher octave. Pentatonic. Valuable practice in accompanying. Pupil could sight read vocal part while teacher plays, and vice versa. Good ear training. Changes in rhythm make the pupil alert. In *B* minor, ending on *D* major. This Hungarian "new" tune is 100 years old—"old" tunes are older!

D. **Suggestions.** In the "new" style, Hungarian tunes are rounded in structure (architectonic in form: AABA, ABBA, etc.) No. 127 is in ABB (varied) A form. "Old" songs are structurally unsymmetrical (ABB, ABCD, ABBC, and so forth).

It is recommended that the pianist should play the **primo** and **secondo** parts of this piece in its transcribed form (see No. 5, **Seven Pieces from "Mikrokosmos"**). See also REMINGTON R19994.

No. 128. Peasant Dance.

A. **Technique.**

   1. TOUCH. **Legato, non-legato, staccato** and **tenuto.**

   2. HAND INDEPENDENCE.

     (a) Counterpoint.

     (b) Combined Touch-Forms: **legato** vs. **non-legato, staccato** and **tenuto.**

     (c) Accompanying Figurations: in L.H.

   3. INTERVAL PLAYING. In each hand. Broken octaves in L.H.

   4. PASSAGE-WORK. Scalar passages in each hand.

   5. EMBELLISHMENTS. Grace notes in R.H.

B. **Musicianship.**

   1. NOTATION. Clef changes in L.H.

   2. RHYTHM. Change of time. Syncopation.

   3. EXPRESSION.

     (a) Tempo: change of tempo.

     (b) Dynamics: accents (>, ∧, *sf, sff*).

     (c) Phrasing: in ternary form.

C. **Bartók's Comments.** An original [Bartók] theme but in old Hungarian modal style. Interesting changes in rhythm and tempo. In the second section, one voice imitates the other. This is symmetrical in form. The ending is a Phrygian cadence. Altered key of *G.*

D. **Suggestions.** The characteristic interval of the Phrygian Mode is the minor second between the first and second degrees. Transposed to *G*:

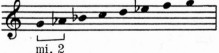

mi. 2

Insofar as the Phrygian cadence is concerned, characteristics are the downward resolution of the minor second and the upward resolution of the seventh, both to the first degree (Tonic).

The Hungarian title means "Stamping Dance." See BR 1:1:4.

No. 129.   Alternating Thirds.

A. **Technique.**

    1. TOUCH. **Non-legato, staccato,** dotted **tenuto** and **tenuto.**

    2. HAND INDEPENDENCE.

       (a) Counterpoint.

       (b) Dynamic Contrast: > vs. *p.*

    3. INTERVAL PLAYING. In each hand.

    4. PASSAGE-WORK. Double thirds.

B. **Musicianship.**

    1. RHYTHM. Subdivision of the beat into two parts: the quarter note as the pulse unit. The quarter note triplet in 2/4 and the half note triplet in 2/2. Change of time. Syncopation.

    2. NOTATION. Clef change in L.H.

    3. EXPRESSION.

       (a) Tempo: **quasi a tempo** = nearly up to tempo.
           tornando al Tempo I = returning to the first speed.

       (b) Dynamics: **leggero** = lightly, without accent.

C. **Bartók's Comments.** This is in Phrygian Mode. Most of the thirds are on white keys. Crisp, but stay very close to keys. Work very carefully on the rhythm at the ending—it must be exact.

D. **Suggestions.** Both triplet figures at the end can be counted by using eighth note and quarter note triplets respectively as frames of reference:

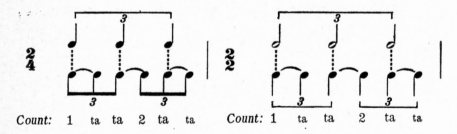

Observe the **diminuendo** in the last seven measures. Bartók's original title was "Scherzo." See BR 1:1:2.

No. 130. Village Joke.

A. **Technique.**

    1. TOUCH. **Legato** and **staccato.**

    2. HAND INDEPENDENCE.

        (a) Combined Touch-Forms: **legato** vs. **staccato.**

        (b) Dynamic Contrasts: $\wedge$ vs. $\boldsymbol{f}$, > vs. $\boldsymbol{p}$.

        (c) Accompanying Figurations: in each hand.

    3. INTERVAL AND CHORD PLAYING. Broken octaves and tenths in L.H. Chords in R.H.

    4. PASSAGE-WORK. Scalar passages in each hand.

    5. EMBELLISHMENTS. Five-note turns in each hand.

    6. FINGERING PROBLEMS. The playing of black key major seconds with R.H. first finger. Chordal and intervallic leaps.

B. **Musicianship.**

    1. NOTATION. Leger-line notes below the staff in the bass clef. Chord cluster notation in the treble clef of m. 27. Mixed accidentals. Change of clef in R.H.

    2. RHYTHM. Subdivision of the beat into five parts: the sixteenth note quintuplet in 2/4. Polyrhythm: five vs. two to the beat.

    3. EXPRESSION.

        (a) Dynamics: **pesante** and **leggero.**

C. **Bartók's Comments.** Lydian Mode. In playing it, make it droll and witty. Upward scales with augmented fourths add to the colorful effect. Also the rhythmic scheme. Note the alterations in the downward scales. Also that the process is reversed from R.H. to L.H. Should be a good concert number or encore.

D. **Suggestions.** Beginning seven measures from the end, be sure to observe all L.H. accents. See BR 2:1:3.

No. 131. Fourths.

A. **Technique.**

    1. TOUCH. **Legato, non-legato, staccato** and **tenuto.**

    2. HAND INDEPENDENCE.

        (a) Combined Touch-Forms: **legato** vs. **staccato.**

3. FINGER INDEPENDENCE. Part-playing in each hand.

4. INTERVAL PLAYING. In each hand. Chord playing in the **Ossia.**

5. EMBELLISHMENTS. Slow tremolos in each hand.

B. **Musicianship.**

1. NOTATION. G♭ key signature. Mixed accidentals. Clef changes in each hand.

2. EXPRESSION.
   (a) Dynamics.

C. **Bartók's Comments.** Contrasts of fourths in G♭ major and E♭ minor. Good example of duo-tonality. Has pentatonic feeling. Accentuation very positive and must be played clearly. Take your choice at the end—whichever preferable.

D. **Suggestions.** Check the part-playing in M. 35-40.

The **Ossia** (which should be played) con-  tains chords built of fourths. Termed quartal harmony (in contrast to the common tertian system in which chords are built of thirds), twentieth-century composers have frequently explored this new structural medium. Indeed, Alexander Scriabin invented this quartal harmony which he called the "Mystic"

chord: Earlier (1908) examples of quartal chords can be found in No. XI of Bartók's **Fourteen Bagatelles** for piano. See BR 1:1:3.

No. 132. Major Seconds Broken and Together.

A. **Technique.**

1. TOUCH. **Legato** and **espressivo.**

2. HAND INDEPENDENCE.
   (a) Counterpoint.
   (b) Combined Touch-Forms: **legato** vs. **espressivo.**

3. FINGER INDEPENDENCE. Part-playing in each hand.
4. FINGERING PROBLEMS. First finger R.H. on two
   keys.
5. INTERVAL AND CHORD PLAYING. In each hand.

B. **Musicianship.**
   1. NOTATION. Treble clef in each hand. Mixed accidentals.
      The solid line (between staves) which indicates that the
      R.H. plays the melody note in the lower staff.
   2. RHYTHM. Change of time: 9/8 and 6/8 as compound
      meters.
   3. EXPRESSION.
      (a) Dynamics: **smorzando** = growing slower and softer.

C. **Bartók's Comments.** Study of chromaticism with a feeling of
G major. Hovering tonality. An exotic effect can be produced.

D. **Suggestions.** The hand contractions required may prove
awkward at first, but use the composer's fingerings to insure a
smooth **legato.** Review the chromatic scale in quick tempo (M.M. ♩
= 120-160).[1]

No. 133. Syncopation.
A. **Technique.**
   1. TOUCH. **Legato** and **non-legato.**
   2. CHORD PLAYING. In each hand.
   3. POSITION. Hand crossings: each hand over and under.
   4. PEDALLING. Use of the damper.
   5. FINGERING PROBLEMS.

B. **Musicianship.**
   1. NOTATION. Clef changes in each hand. Bass clef leger-
      line notes below the staff. Mixed accidentals. **8ᵛᵉ· bassa**
      in L.H.
   2. RHYTHM. Change of time: 5/4, 3/4, 4/4. Syncopation.
   3. EXPRESSION.
      (a) Dynamics: **pesante,** accents, ***pp-ff.***

C. **Bartók's Comments.** Difficult rhythmic patterns require close
study. Not for average pupil. Key of G. Good preparation for
Prokofiev.

1See p. 80.

D. **Suggestions.** Note the held tones in M. 14-17 (R.H.).

See BR 1:4:1.

No. 134.   Studies in Double Notes (1) (2) (3).

  A. **Technique.**

    1. TOUCH. **Legato** and **staccato.**

    2. HAND INDEPENDENCE.
      (a) Dynamic Contrast: **crescendo** vs. **diminuendo.**

    3. INTERVAL PLAYING. In each hand.

    4. EMBELLISHMENTS. Double-note tremolos and grace notes in each hand.

    5. FINGERING PROBLEMS.

  B. **Musicianship.**

    1. NOTATION. Mixed accidentals. Clef changes in each hand.

    2. EXPRESSION.
      (a) Dynamics.

C. **Bartók's Comments.** Excellent preparation for all fast double-note playing. Could be practised in different rhythms, **staccato,** etc. Very valuable to develop a firm hold upon the keys.

D. **Suggestions.** The third study can be used for the practice of hand independence: **legato** vs. **staccato** and dotted eighth—sixteenth note patterns vs. eighth note patterns as written.

According to the Hungarian title, a better heading for this piece would be "Studies in Double Stops."

No. 135.   Perpetuum Mobile.

A. **Technique.**

1. TOUCH. **Legato.**
2. INTERVAL PLAYING. In each hand.
3. POSITION. Hand crossing: L.H. over.
4. EMBELLISHMENTS. Double-note tremolos in each hand.
5. FINGERING PROBLEMS.

B. **Musicianship.**

1. NOTATION. Clef changes in L.H. Mixed accidentals.
2. EXPRESSION.
   (a) Terms: **repet. ad infinitum** = repeat indefinitely.

C. **Bartók's Comments.** Excellent technical work in chromatic double notes in repetition. Altered key of *F*.

D. **Suggestions. Perpetuum Mobile** = perpetual motion = a piece which proceeds from beginning to end in the same rapid motion. A two-piano transcription of this piece appears as no. 3 in **Seven Pieces from "Mikrokosmos".**

No. 136.   Whole-Tone Scale.

A. **Technique.**

1. TOUCH. **Legato** and **espressivo (dolce, cantabile).**
2. HAND INDEPENDENCE.
   (a) Counterpoint.
3. FINGER INDEPENDENCE. Part-playing in each hand.
4. CHORD PLAYING. In each hand.

5. POSITION. Hand crossings: R.H. and L.H. over and under.

6. EMBELLISHMENTS. Five-note turn in L.H.

B. **Musicianship.**

1. NOTATION. Mixed accidentals. Clef changes in each hand.

2. RHYTHM. The eighth note quintuplet in 2/4. Change of time.

3. EXPRESSION.
   (a) Tempo: change of tempo. **Marcato.**
   (b) Dynamics.
   (c) Phrasing: separating signs. Canonic rondo-variation form.
   (d) Terms: **stringendo** = growing faster and louder.

C. **Bartók's Comments.** Whole-tone scales

of *C*   and *A*

in juxtaposition, worked out in many other keys, in changed rhythms and tempos. These devices are used to produce color.

D. **Suggestions.** Note the separating signs which interrupt the **legato** in M. 34, 40 and 49.

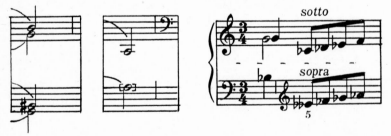

Observe that the quintuplet in m. 79 is to be played **sempre più lento.** See BR 2:5:1.

No. 137.   Unison.

A. **Technique.**

    1. TOUCH. **Legato, legatissimo, tenuto** and **espressivo.**

    2. HAND INDEPENDENCE.

        (a) Combined Touch-Forms: **legato** vs. **espressivo.**

    3. FINGERING PROBLEMS.

    4. POSITION. The hands two, three, and four octaves apart. Playing in extreme ranges of the keyboard.

B. **Musicianship.**

    1. NOTATION. Leger-line notes in each clef. Clef changes in each hand. *D* key signature.

    2. RHYTHM. Change of time: 2/4, 3/4, 5/8, 6/8, 7/8.

    3. EXPRESSION.

        (a) Tempo: **lunga** = long = the tone should be held (here) for at least double the value of the note. Change of tempo.

        (b) Dynamics: *pp* to *ff.*

        (c) Terms: **ma sonoro** = but with a sonorous or ringing tone.

        (d) Phrasing: in ternary form.

C. **Bartók's Comments.** Excellent practice for reading, making quick changes of position, meter changes, clef signs, and style (dynamics and touch). Key of *D.*

D. **Suggestions.**
Legatissimo (M. 50-54) "is an exaggerated **legato:** when every tone is held over a little into the beginning of the next one. It can be perfected by using the half-pedal."

No. 138.   Bagpipe.

A. **Technique.**

    1. TOUCH. **Legato, non-legato, staccato** and **tenuto.**

2. HAND INDEPENDENCE.
   (a) Combined Touch-Forms: **non-legato** vs. **legato, staccato** and **tenuto.**
   (b) Dynamic Contrast: **_p_** vs. _mf,_ > vs. **_p._** and _mf._
   (c) Accompanying Figurations: in L.H.
3. FINGER INDEPENDENCE. Part-playing in each hand.
4. PEDALLING. Optional use of the damper.
5. PASSAGE-WORK. Scalar passages in R.H.
6. EMBELLISHMENTS. Three and five-note trills in rapid tempo (R.H. only).

B. **Musicianship.**
1. NOTATION. Clef changes in L.H.
2. RHYTHM. Subdivision of the beat into two, five, six, and seven parts: the quarter note as the pulse unit in 2/4 and 3/4. The sixteenth note triplet, quintuplet, sextuplet, and septuplet. Polyrhythm: five vs. two.
3. EXPRESSION.
   (a) Tempo: change of tempo.
   (b) Dynamics.
   (c) Phrasing: in ternary form.

C. **Bartók's Comments.** Use of all three pipes: chanter, tonic and dominant, and the drone. Interesting division of the pipes. Squeaky effects are typical. It never ends normally because the air is going out of the pipes. Accent first beat of the five-note groupings.

D. **Suggestions.** M. 1-27 exemplify Bartók's use of non-coinciding meters: the L.H. is in 3/8 and the R.H. is in 2/4 meter.

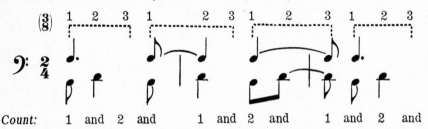

The pipes are divided as follows: soprano voice = chanter, alto voice = drone pipe, and the bass and tenor voices = the tonic-dominant pipe. Be sure that _a_ is held down in the last two measures (R.H.).

No. 139.   Merry Andrew.

A. **Technique.**

    1. TOUCH. **Legato, non-legato, staccato, tenuto** and dotted **tenuto.**

    2. HAND INDEPENDENCE.
       (a) Counterpoint.
       (b) Combined Touch-Forms: **legato** vs. **staccato, non-legato, tenuto,** and dotted **tenuto, non-legato** and **tenuto** vs. **staccato.**
       (c) Dynamic Contrast: $\wedge$ vs. f.

    3. FINGER INDEPENDENCE. Part-playing in L.H.

    4. INTERVAL, CHORD, AND BROKEN CHORD PLAYING. In each hand.

    5. POSITION. Interlocked hands. Hand crossings: R.H. and L.H. over.

    6. PASSAGE-WORK. Scalar passages in R.H.

    7. FINGERING PROBLEMS.

B. **Musicianship.**

    1. NOTATION. Clef changes in R.H., treble clef in L.H.

    2. EXPRESSION.
       (a) Dynamics.

C. **Bartók's Comments.** Changes in key and tonality create a gay, droll effect. Major against minor in certain places. Key of C.

D. **Suggestions. Paprikajancsi** $=$ Jack-Pudding or Harlequin: a buffoon or clownish fellow. See BR 2:1:4.

Nos. 140-153

No. 140.   Free Variations.

A.   Technique.

1. TOUCH. **Legato, non-legato, staccato** and **tenuto.**

2. HAND INDEPENDENCE.
   (a) Counterpoint.
   (b) Combined Touch-Forms: **non-legato** vs. **tenuto** and **staccato, legato** vs. **tenuto.**
   (c) Dynamic Contrasts: p vs. mf, $\wedge$ vs. f.
   (d) Accompanying Figurations: in each hand.

3. INTERVAL, CHORD, AND BROKEN CHORD PLAYING. In each hand.

4. FINGER INDEPENDENCE. Part-playing in L.H.

5. PEDALLING. Use of the half-depressed damper.

6. PASSAGE-WORK. Rapid scalar passage in R.H.

7. FINGERING PROBLEMS.

B.   Musicianship.

1. NOTATION. Clef changes in each hand.

2. RHYTHM. Subdivision of the beat into eight parts: the quarter note as the pulse unit in 2/4. Change of time: 2/4, 3/8, 4/8, 5/8, 6/8, 7/8, 8/8, and 9/8. Syncopation. 9/8 as compound triple meter and as additive rhythm $\frac{(4+3+2)}{8}$. 7/8 as $\frac{4+3}{8}$ and 8/8 as $\frac{3+3+2}{8}$.

3. EXPRESSION.
   (a) Tempo: change of tempo. **Il doppio più lento** $=$ twice as slow. **Stretto** $=$ quicker.
   (b) Dynamics: **intenso** $=$ with intensity, stress.
   (c) Terms: **lugubre** $=$ mournfully. **Strepitoso** $=$ noisily.
   (d) Phrasing: in rondo-variation form.

    C.   **Bartók's Comments.** Ingenious variety of treatment. Change of mood, change of tempo and style. Excellent technical and rhythmic materials.

D. **Suggestions.** Observe the separating sign (comma) in m. 12. Begin m. 44 at M.M. ♩ = 80.

Il doppio
più lento

See BR 1:3:3.

No. 141. Subject and Reflection.

A. **Technique.**
   1. TOUCH. **Legato, non-legato, staccato** and **tenuto.**
   2. HAND INDEPENDENCE.
      (a) Combined Touch-Forms: **legato** vs. **tenuto.**
   3. FINGER INDEPENDENCE. Part-playing in each hand.
   4. POSITION. Crossing of the hands: R.H. under.

B. **Musicianship.**
   1. NOTATION. Clef changes in each hand. Leger-line notes above the staff in the treble and below the staff in the bass clef. Mixed accidentals.
   2. RHYTHM. Change of time: 2/4, 3/4, 3/8, 5/8, 7/8. Syncopation.
   3. EXPRESSION.
      (a) Tempo: change of tempo: **Vivacissimo** = very quick.
      (b) Phrasing: in rondo-variation form.
      (c) Dynamics: accents.

C. **Bartók's Comments.** Subject clearly defined and arranged in changing meters, keys, and styles of tonality. Tonality is B♭. I think of this as being mirrored in water: as the water becomes disturbed the reflection becomes distorted.

D. **Suggestions.** Observe the slight pause indicated by the separating sign in m. 22. See BR 2:4:3.

No. 142.   From the Diary of a Fly.

A.   Technique.

1. TOUCH. **Legato, non-legato, staccato** and **tenuto.**

2. HAND INDEPENDENCE.
   (a) Counterpoint.
   (b) Combined Touch-Forms: **legato** vs. **staccato.**
   (c) Dynamic Contrast: *sf* vs. *mf.*

3. FINGER INDEPENDENCE. Part-playing in each hand.
   Combined touch-forms: in M. 44-45 the soprano voice is **non-legato** and the alto voice is **staccato.**

In M. 44-46 the tenor voice is **staccato** and the bass voice is **non-legato.**

In M. 46-48 the soprano voice is **tenuto** and the alto voice is **staccato.** In M. 47-48 the tenor voice is **staccato** and the bass voice is **tenuto.**

Dynamic contrast: in M. 42-43

and alto voice is **marcatissimo** and in M. 44-48 the soprano and bass voices are similarly accented. In m. 43 the tenor voice is **marcatissimo** and in the next measure it is **marcato** at the same time the bass voice is **marcatissimo.**

4. POSITION. Interlocked hands. Hand crossings: R.H. and L.H. over and under.

5. CHORD PLAYING. In each hand.

6. EMBELLISHMENTS. Trills and tremolos in each hand.

B. **Musicianship.**

1. NOTATION. Mixed accidentals. Treble clef in each hand.

2. RHYTHM. Change of time. Syncopation.

3. EXPRESSION.
    (a) Tempo: change of tempo. **Agitato** = agitated. **Poco stringendo** = a little acceleration and increase in intensity.
    (b) Dynamics: *sff, sf.* ∧ , >. **Leggero.**
    (c) Terms: **lamentoso** = in a melancholy, sad style. **con gioia** = joyfully.
    (d) Phrasing: in ternary form.

C. **Bartók's Comments.** I wanted to depict the desperate sound of a fly's buzz, when getting into a cob-web. The fly is telling the story as he writes in his diary. He was buzzing about and didn't see the spider web. Then he is caught in the web (**Agitato**: "Woe, a cobweb!"), but he manages to get himself free before he is eaten, and he escapes. A happy ending (**con gioia**). Play it delicately, close to the keys. *Slight* use of wrist in **staccato,** it must be flexible.

D. **Suggestions.** Take notice of the slight pause in m. 59

con gioia

and the replacement of fingers in L.H. of M. 72-73.

poco cresc.

Note also the ties in M. 75-87 and 98-102.

See BR 1:3:2.

No. 143. Divided Arpeggios.

A. **Technique.**

1. TOUCH. **Legato, non-legato, staccato, tenuto** and **espressivo.**

2. HAND INDEPENDENCE.
    (a) Counterpoint.

3. FINGER INDEPENDENCE. Part-playing in each hand.

4. CHORD AND BROKEN CHORD PLAYING. In each hand.

5. POSITION. Hand crossings: L.H. and R.H. over and under.

6. PEDALLING. Use of the damper.

7. PASSAGE-WORK. Rapid arpeggios (without passing of the fingers) in each hand.

B. **Musicianship.**

1. NOTATION. Clef changes in each hand. Mixed accidentals. Treble clef leger-line notes above and below the staff.

2. RHYTHM. Change of time: 2/4, 1/4. Syncopation.

3. EXPRESSION.
   (a) Tempo: change of tempo. **Un poco stentato** = retarding a little.
   (b) Dynamics: **mezza voce** = *mf.*

C. **Bartók's Comments.** This is very difficult for average pupils to play and understand. The themes must be introduced clearly and with great care for rhythmic accuracy. Only for unusual pupils.

D. **Suggestions.** Use **espressivo** touch in M. 27-28 only. The arpeggios are broken chords in five finger positions which do not require passing of the fingers. See BR 2:2:1.

No. 144.   Minor Seconds, Major Sevenths.

A. **Technique.**
   1. TOUCH. **Legato, non-legato, staccato, tenuto** and **portamento (portato).**
   2. HAND INDEPENDENCE.
      (a) Counterpoint.
      (b) Combined Touch-Forms: **tenuto** vs. dotted **tenuto** and **portamento.**
   3. FINGER INDEPENDENCE. Part-playing in each hand.
   4. INTERVAL, CHORD, AND BROKEN CHORD PLAYING. In each hand.
   5. POSITION. Interlocked hands. Hand crossings: L.H. over.
   6. PASSAGE-WORK. Scalar and arpeggio passages in each hand.
   7. PEDALLING. Indicated and optional use of the damper.
   8. FINGERING PROBLEMS.

B. **Musicianship.**
   1. NOTATION. Clef changes in each hand. Thirty-second notes and double-dotted eighth and quarter notes. Mixed accidentals.
   2. RHYTHM. Subdivision of the beat into eight parts: the quarter note as the pulse unit in 4/4. Change of time: 4/4, 2/4 and 3/2. Syncopation.

3. EXPRESSION.
  (a) Tempo: change of tempo. **Doppio movimento** = twice
      as fast.
  (b) Dynamics: **intenso.**
  (c) Terms: **mesto** = pensive, melancholy.

C. **Bartók's Comments.** This is very difficult and requires a pupil
who has great control. The sevenths are bells and they emphasize
the melody.

D. **Suggestions.** Note the **decrescendo** that takes place towards
each dotted eighth note (m. 1ff.).

In m. 38 the L.H. crosses over to play *d* an octave higher than the
leger-line *d* in the R.H.

In m. 41 the *e* natural and *e♭* played by the L.H. should be released
on b. 3 and, in M. 41-42, observe the tied notes in the R.H. See
BR 2:3:1.

No. 145. Chromatic Invention.

A. **Technique.**

1. TOUCH. **Non-legato** and **tenuto.**

2. HAND INDEPENDENCE.
   (a) Counterpoint.
   (b) Combined Touch-Forms: **non-legato** vs. **tenuto.**
   (c) Dynamic Contrasts: >, ∧, and *sf.*

3. INTERVAL PLAYING. Octaves in each hand.

4. POSITION. Hand crossings: R.H. and L.H. over, L.H. under.

5. ENSEMBLE PLAYING. Parts "a" and "b" together as a piece for two pianos.

B. **Musicianship.**

1. NOTATION. Clef changes in each hand. Mixed accidentals.

2. RHYTHM. Change of time. Syncopation.

3. EXPRESSION.
   (a) Tempo: **accelerando sin al fine** = increasing in speed up to the end.
   (b) Dynamics: *fff* = extremely loud.
   (c) Terms: **con 8 (ad lib.)** = with octaves (if the performer wishes to do so).

C. **Bartók's Comments.** Versions "a" and "b" can be played separately, or together on two pianos.

D. **Suggestions.** The two-piano transcription of this piece in **Seven Pieces from "Mikrokosmos"** (no. 6) contains part "a" as the **primo** and part "b" as the **secondo.** See REMINGTON R19994.

No. 146. Ostinato.

A. **Technique.**

1. TOUCH. **Legato, non-legato, tenuto,** dotted **tenuto, staccato** and **staccatissimo.**

2. HAND INDEPENDENCE.
   (a) Combined Touch-Forms: **legato** vs. **non-legato** and **tenuto. Non-legato** vs. **tenuto, staccato** and **staccatissimo.**
   (b) Dynamic Contrasts: >, ∧, and *sf.*

(c) Accompanying Figurations: L.H. only.

3. FINGER INDEPENDENCE. Part-playing in each hand.
4. INTERVAL AND CHORD PLAYING. In each hand.
   Also octaves, and chords with the span of an octave.
5. PEDALLING. Use of the damper.
6. POSITION. Hand crossings: L.H. and R.H. over.
7. PASSAGE-WORK. Scalar passages in each hand.
8. FINGERING PROBLEMS.

B. **Musicianship.**
   1. NOTATION. Clef changes in each hand. Mixed accidentals. Leger-line notes in each clef.
   2. RHYTHM. Syncopation.
   3. EXPRESSION.
      (a) Tempo: change of tempo. **Non accelerando (non acc.), meno vivo.**
      (b) Dynamics: **leggero.**

C. **Bartók's Comments. Ostinato:** a ground bass which recurs obstinately throughout the composition. Has a definite Oriental feeling. Dorian Mode with alterations. This is not actually a traditional **ostinato,** because the traditional **ostinato** was a repeated theme. Also suggests Bulgarian pipes on page seventeen [m. 32ff.].

D. **Suggestions.** Take notice of the **staccatissimo** marks in the R.H. of M. 138, 142 and 145.

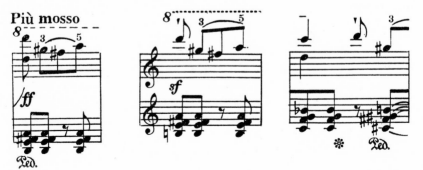

In m. 154, b. 1, the octave of *d* can be divided between the hands.

A transcription of this piece appears as no. 7 in **Seven Pieces from "Mikrokosmos"**. Although the piece is listed on the back jacket of Bartók's recording of the **Mikrokosmos** (Columbia ML4419), it does not appear in the record itself.

No. 147.   March.

A. **Technique.**

1. TOUCH. **Legato, non-legato, tenuto, staccato** and **staccatissimo.**

2. HAND INDEPENDENCE.
   (a) Combined Touch-Forms: **legato** vs. **non-legato, tenuto** and **staccato. Tenuto** vs. **non-legato** and **staccato.**
   (b) Dynamic Contrasts: ∧ and *sf.*
   (c) Accompanying Figurations: in each hand.

3. FINGER INDEPENDENCE. Part-playing in each hand.

4. INTERVAL AND CHORD PLAYING. In each hand.

5. POSITION. Hand crossing: R.H. over.

6. PASSAGE-WORK. Octaves in each hand.

7. EMBELLISHMENTS. Octave trill in R.H.

8. FINGERING PROBLEMS.

B. **Musicianship.**

1. NOTATION. Mixed accidentals. Clef changes in R.H.

2. RHYTHM. Change of time: 4/4, 5/4, 3/2. Subdivision of the beat into two, three, and four parts: the quarter note as the pulse unit in 4/4.

3. EXPRESSION.
   (a) Dynamics: *sf* and other accents. *fff.*
   (b) Terms: **sonoro.**

C. Bartók's Comments. Repetition in L.H. (fourths and fifths) creates a grotesque effect—like a march of primitive peoples.

D. Suggestions. This piece requires quick hand crossings and judicious use of the damper pedal. In m. 26 the separating sign interrupts the **legato** (L.H.).

Note the fingerings in M. 31-32 and that f♯ is tied over the next three bars.

The practice of chromatic octaves could be undertaken here.

The solo **sostenuto** pedal can be used in M. 54-55. See BR 2:2:2.

No. 148. Six Dances in Bulgarian Rhythm (1).

A. Technique.

1. TOUCH. **Legato, non-legato, tenuto,** dotted **tenuto, staccato, portamento** and **espressivo (dolce).**

2. HAND INDEPENDENCE.
   (a) Counterpoint.
   (b) Combined Touch-Forms: **legato** vs. **non-legato, staccato, tenuto,** dotted **tenuto** and **portamento.** Dotted **tenuto** vs. **portamento. Staccato** and **non-legato. Espressivo** vs. **legato,** dotted **tenuto** and **portamento.**
   (c) Dynamic Contrast: > vs. ∧.
   (d) Accompanying Figurations: in each hand.

3. FINGER INDEPENDENCE. Part-playing in each hand.

4. INTERVAL, CHORD, AND BROKEN CHORD PLAYING. Octaves in each hand and tenths in L.H. Arpeggiated triads in L.H. Chords with the span of an octave and a ninth.

5. POSITION. Interlocked hands: L.H. under.

6. PASSAGE-WORK. Scalar passages in each hand.

7. EMBELLISHMENTS. Grace notes, turns, and the **Pralltriller** (inverted mordent) in R.H.

8. FINGERING PROBLEMS.

B. Musicianship.

1. NOTATION. Clef changes in each hand. The inverted mordent. Mixed accidentals.

2. RHYTHM. Additive rhythm: $\frac{4+2+3}{8}$. Syncopation.

3. EXPRESSION.
   (a) Dynamics: **rinf.** = **rinforzato** = a sudden increase in loudness (in this short passage).
   (b) Phrasing: in variation form.

C. **Bartók's Comments.** Hexachord in Dorian Mode, repeated in the left hand, which never goes to the octave in range. Changes in accentuation typical of Bulgarian rhythm. The phrase dictated the meter sign, because of accentuation. Odd-numbered groups heavily accented.

D. **Suggestions.** The ascending scalar passages in the L.H. of

M. 4ff. are fingered

and the soprano voice in m. 34 can be played

The inverted mordents are played as illustrated:
m. 38,   m. 48,

m. 52

Do not play them as sixteenth note triplets or as grace notes in anticipation of the beat. Pianists with small hands may play the tenth in M. 33 and 52

as broken intervals. The last chord in m. 55 can be shared between the hands.

No. 149.   Six Dances in Bulgarian Rhythm (2)

A. **Technique.**

   1. TOUCH. **Legato, non-legato, staccato, tenuto** and dotted **tenuto.**

   2. HAND INDEPENDENCE.
      (a) Counterpoint.
      (b) Combined Touch-Forms: **legato** vs. **staccato** and dotted **tenuto. Non-legato** vs. **tenuto.**
      (c) Dynamic Contrasts: > vs. **p** and ∧ . *sff* vs. ∧ , ∧ vs. *mf.*
      (d) Accompanying Figurations: in each hand.

3. FINGER INDEPENDENCE. Part-playing in each hand.

4. INTERVAL AND CHORD PLAYING. In each hand.

5. PEDALLING. Optional use of the damper.

6. PASSAGE-WORK. Scalar passages in each hand.

7. EMBELLISHMENTS. Slow trill in R.H.

B. **Musicianship.**

1. NOTATION. Clef changes in each hand.

2. RHYTHM. Additive rhythm: $\frac{2+2+3}{8}$

3. EXPRESSION.

(a) Dynamics: **martellato** $=$ hammering $=$ a percussive **staccato** touch played **forte** or louder.

Usually requires the use of the forearm to achieve the indicated dynamic level.

C. **Bartók's Comment.** The rhythmic figure in the first measure is very important—maintained throughout.

D. **Suggestions.** The value of the eighth note is M.M.=120. See BR 1:4:2.

No. 150.   Six Dances in Bulgarian Rhythm (3).

A. **Technique.**

1. TOUCH. **Legato, non-legato, tenuto, staccato** and **staccatissimo.**

2. HAND INDEPENDENCE.

(a) Counterpoint.

(b) Combined Touch-Forms: **legato** vs. **tenuto** and **non-legato. Tenuto** vs. **non-legato.**

(c) Dynamic Contrast: $\wedge$ vs. f and $>$ vs. p.

(d) Accompanying Figurations: in L.H.

3. FINGER INDEPENDENCE. Part-playing in each hand. Dynamic contrast: $\wedge$ in the bass voice (M. 37, 41).

4. INTERVAL PLAYING. **Legato** sixths in L.H.

5. POSITION. Hand crossing: R.H. under.

6. EMBELLISHMENTS. Grace note in L.H.

7. FINGERING PROBLEMS.

B. **Musicianship.**

   1. NOTATION. Clef change in L.H. Mixed accidentals.

   2. RHYTHM. Additive rhythm: $\dfrac{2+3\ (5/8)}{8}$.

   3. EXPRESSION.

     (a) Tempo: change of tempo.

     (b) Dynamics: **marcato** and **leggero.**

     (c) Phrasing: canonic form in M. 58-78.

C. **Bartók's Comments.** 5/8 time. Very much like other things written before it.

D. **Suggestions.** Play **staccatissimo** on b.2 of m.4 in both

hands.  Use of the solo **sostenuto** pedal (or damper

pedal) will be required for the L.H. beginning in

m. 35 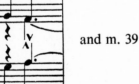 and m. 39

Play the **leggero** sections without emphasis except as marked, and interrupt the **legato** as indicated by the comma between M. 92 and 93. The value of the eighth notes is M.M. = 400. See BR 1:5:2.

No. 151.   Six Dances in Bulgarian Rhythm (4).

A. **Technique.**
   1. TOUCH. **Legato, non-legato, tenuto** and dotted **tenuto.**
   2. HAND INDEPENDENCE.
      (a) Counterpoint.
      (b) Combined Touch-Forms: **non-legato** vs. **tenuto** and dotted **tenuto.**
      (c) Accompanying Figurations: in each hand.
   3. INTERVAL AND CHORD PLAYING. In each hand. Octaves in R.H.
   4. POSITION. Interlocked hands: R.H. over.
   5. PASSAGE. Chordal passages in L.H.
   6. EMBELLISHMENTS. Grace notes and fast trills in each hand.
   7. FINGERING PROBLEMS. Repeated notes.

B. **Musicianship.**
   1. NOTATION. Clef changes in each hand. Mixed accidentals. The trill sign.
   2. RHYTHM. Additive rhythm: $\frac{3+2+3}{8}$. Syncopation.
   3. EXPRESSION.
      (a) Tempo: change of tempo.
      (b) Dynamics.
      (c) Phrasing: in variation form.

C. **Bartók's Comments.** Very much in the style of Gershwin. Gershwin's tonality, rhythm, and color. American folk song feeling. Moderate tempo but vital, crisp, and accented.

D. **Suggestions.** Bartók, in his recording of this piece, accents each quarter note of the melody (R.H. beginning m. 1).

Note the separating sign (comma) in m. 50

and the **fermata** between the last two bars.

Note change in rhythm on B. 1-3 in M. 22-23.

See BR 1:5:3.

No. 152.   Six Dances in Bulgarian Rhythm (5).

A. **Technique.**

1. TOUCH. **Legato, non-legato, staccato** and **tenuto.**
2. HAND INDEPENDENCE.
   (a) Counterpoint.
   (b) Combined Touch-Forms: **legato** vs. **non-legato, staccato** and **tenuto.**
   (c) Accompanying Figurations: in each hand.
3. FINGER INDEPENDENCE. Part-playing in each hand.

4. INTERVAL AND CHORD PLAYING. In each hand.

5. POSITION. Hand crossings: R.H. and L.H. over.

6. EMBELLISHMENTS. Slow trills in both hands and fast trills in R.H.

B. **Musicianship.**

1. NOTATION. Clef changes in each hand. Mixed accidentals.

2. RHYTHM. Additive rhythm: $\dfrac{2+2+2+3}{8}$. Syncopation.

3. EXPRESSION.
   (a) Dynamics: **leggero.**

C. **Bartók's Comments.** Combination of **staccato** and **legato.** Mixed key, ending in *A*. Rhythm—strong accents.

D. **Suggestions.**

L.H. **sopra** in M. 7-10

and R.H. **sopra** in M. 11-15. See BR 1:6:2.

No. 153.   Six Dances in Bulgarian Rhythm (6).

A. **Technique.**

1. TOUCH. **Legato** and **non-legato** playing.

2. HAND INDEPENDENCE.

3. FINGER INDEPENDENCE. Part-playing in each hand.
   (a) Counterpoint.
   (b) Combined Touch-Forms: **legato** vs. **staccato.**

(c) Dynamic Contrasts: ∧ vs. *f* and *sf* vs. *f*. **Marc.** **(marcato)** vs. *f*.

(d) Accompanying Figurations: in each hand.

3. FINGER INDEPENDENCE. Part-playing in each hand.

4. INTERVAL AND CHORD PLAYING. In each hand. Octave and broken octave playing in each hand.

5. PASSAGE-WORK. Scalar passages in each hand.

6. FINGERING PROBLEMS. Repeated notes.

7. PEDALLING. Use of the damper.

B. **Musicianship.**

1. NOTATION. Clef changes in each hand. Mixed accidentals.

2. RHYTHM. Additive rhythm: $\frac{3+3+2}{8}$. Syncopation.

3. EXPRESSION.

(a) Dynamics: **marcato, marcatissimo.**

(b) Phrasing: canonic writing M. 25-29. In ternary form.

(c) Terms: **strepitoso** = noisily.

C. **Bartók's Comments.** Polytonal—chords against organ point. Key of *E*. Especially third group of each measure accented.

Bring out accents in left hand of m. 9ff. Buzzing effect in m. 69ff.

   D. Suggestions. In m. 49 middle *c* should be played with the thumb of the R.H.

The repeated notes in M. 81-82 can be fingered:

Avoid accentuation in the **leggero** section (m. 75ff.).

See BR 1:6:3.

AMERINGER, SILVIA. "Teaching with Bartók's 'Mikrokosmos'," **Tempo** (London), Autumn, 1951.

ANONYMOUS. "Béla Bartók's **Mikrokosmos**." **Tempo** (New York), April, 1940.

———————— **Introducing Béla Bartók.** London: Boosey and Hawkes, 1955.

AUSTIN, WILLIAM W. **Music in the 20th Century.** New York: W.W. Norton, 1966.

BALOGH, ERNÖ. "Bartók, The Teacher—As I Knew Him." **Etude,** January, 1956.

BARNA, ISTVÁN. "Bartók Változatok." **Énekszó** (Budapest), March, 1950.

BARTÓK, BÉLA. **Preface and Notes to Mikrokosmos.** New York: Boosey and Hawkes, 1940, Vols. I-IV.

———————— "The Influence of Peasant Music on Modern Music." **A Memorial Review** (Boosey and Hawkes, New York), 1950.

———————— **101 Essays** (edited by Benjamin Suchoff). London: Faber and Faber, 1971.

———————— **Rumanian Folk Music** (edited by Benjamin Suchoff). The Hague: Martinus Nijhoff, 1967 (Vol. I-III), 1971 (Vols. IV-V).

———————— and RESCHOFSKY, SANDOR. **Zongora Iskola.** Budapest: Rózsavölgyi és Társa, 1913. (**Piano Method:** English Edition ed. Leslie Russell, London: Boosey and Hawkes, 1968).

BATOR, VICTOR, **The Bartók Archives: History and Catalogue.** New York: Bartók Archives Studies in Musicology, No. 1, 1963.

BENARY, PETER. "Die zweistimmige Kontrapunkt in Bartóks 'Mikrokosmos'." **Archiv für Musikwissenschaft** (Trossingen), 1958.

BÓNIS, FERENC. **Béla Bartók: His Life in Pictures.** Budapest: Corvina Press, 1964.

BULL, STORM. "Bartók the Teacher." **Musical Facts** (Chicago), March, 1941.

———————— "Bartók's Teaching Pieces." **Repertoire** (Lansing), October, 1951.

CHASINS, ABRAM. "Etude on Etudes . . . the 'Mikrokosmos' of Béla Bartók." **Saturday Review,** June 30, 1956.

DALLIN, LEON. **Techniques of Twentieth Century Composition.** Dubuque: Wm. C. Brown, 1957.

DAVIS, MAXINE C. **Analytical Study of the Mikrokosmos of Béla Bartók.** Doctor's thesis, Columbia University, 1957.

DEMÉNY, JÁNOS. **Bartók Béla a zongoraművész.** Budapest: Zeneműkiadó Vallalat, 1968.

DILLE, DENIJS, editor. **Documenta Bartókiana.** Budapest: Akadémiai Kiadó, 1964 (Vol. I), 1965 (Vol. II), 1968 (Vol. III).

DOFLEIN, ERICH. "Bartók und die Musikpädagogik." **Musik der Zeit** (Bonn), 1953, Heft III.

———————— "Über Bartók's 'Mikrokosmos'." **Melos** (Mainz), July-August, 1954.

DOWNES, OLIN. **The New York Times,** 25 April, 1940.

DOWNEY, JOHN. **La Musique Populaire dans l'Oeuvre de Béla Bartók.** Paris: Publication No. 5 of the Musicological Institute of the University of Paris, 1966.

DUSTIN, WILLIAM D. **Two-Voiced Textures in the Mikrokosmos of Béla Bartók.** Doctor's thesis, Cornell University, 1959.

ENGEL, IVAN. "A- 'Mikrokosmos'-ról." **Zenei Szemle** (Budapest), December, 1948.

———————————— "A Mikrokosmos a Gyakorlatban." **Zenei Szemle,** October, 1955.

ENGELMANN, HANS ULRICH. **Béla Bartók's Mikrokosmos: Versuch einer Typologie "Neuer Musik."** Würzburg: Konrad Triltsch, 1953.

———————————— "Chromatische Ausstufung in Béla Bartók's 'Mikrokosmos'." **Melos,** May, 1951.

FARKAS, FERENC. "Bartók Mikrokosmosa." **A Zene** (Budapest), 1940.

FASSETT, AGATHA. **The Naked Face of Genius.** Boston: Houghton Mifflin Company, 1958.

FENYO, THOMAS. **The Piano Music of Béla Bartók.** Doctor's thesis, University of California at Los Angeles, 1956.

FOLDES, ANDOR. "Bartók as Pianist." **Juilliard Review,** Fall, 1955.

———————————— "Béla Bartók's Piano Works." **Listen,** January, 1946.

———————————— "Béla Bartók." **Tempo** (London), No. 43, 1957.

FÖLDESSY, LULA H. "Bartók Béla Mikrokosmos-áról." **Magyar Zenei Szemle** (Budapest), April, 1941.

FRANKENSTEIN, ALFRED. "Bartók on Microgroove," **High Fidelity,** October, 1956.

FRISKIN, J. and FREUNDLICH, I. **Music for the Piano.** New York: Rinehart, 1954.

GERAEDTS, HENRI. **Béla Bartók.** Haarlem-Antwerpen: J. H. Gottmer, 1952.

HERNADI, LAJOS. "Béla Bartók, Le Pianiste, Le Pédagogue, L'homme." **La Revue Musicale** (Paris), No. 224, 1955.

HOLCMAN, JAN. "Bartók á la Chinese Torture." **Saturday Review,** October 13, 1956.

HORAN, MOTHER M. ANNUNCIATA. **The Mikrokosmos of Béla Bartók.** Doctor's thesis, Boston University, 1957.

HORN, HERBERT A. **Idiomatic Writing of the Piano Music of Béla Bartók.** Doctor's thesis, University of Southern California, 1963.

MASON, COLIN. "Béla Bartók's 'Mikrokosmos'." **Music Teacher and Piano Student** (London), February, 1946.

MIDDLETON, JEAN B. "Teaching Pieces by Béla Bartók." **Piano Quarterly Newsletter** (New York), Winter, 1954-5.

MILA, MASSIMO. "Béla Bartók ed il suo 'Mikrokosmos'." **Il Diapason** (Milan), 1950.

MOREUX, SERGE. **Bartók.** London: Harvill Press, 1953.

NOVIK, YLDA. "Teaching with 'Mikrokosmos'." **Tempo** (London), No. 83' 1968.

OGDON, JOHN, "Bartók's **Mikrokosmos**." **Tempo** (London), No. 65, 1963.

OLLIER, CL. "Béla Bartók et **Mikrokosmos**." **Revue de la Mediterranée** (Paris), Vol. VIII, No. 3, 1950.

PARRISH, DOROTHY. "Teaching Pieces by Béla Bartók." **Piano Quarterly Newsletter**, Winter, 1954-5.

PERKINS, FRANCIS D. Review in **New York Herald Tribune**, 25 April, 1940.

PERSICHETTI, VINCENT. **Twentieth-Century Harmony**. New York: W. W. Norton, 1961.

REDLICH, HANS. "Seven Pieces from **Mikrokosmos**. Arranged for Two Pianos, Four Hands." **Music Review** (London), Vol. IX, No. 3, 1948.

REHBERG, ZOLETTE. "Une Education Musicale Nouvelle." **Connaître** (Geneva), March, 1952.

RIEFLING, REIMAR. **Piano Pedalling**. London: Oxford University Press, 1962.

ROTHE, FRIEDE F. "The Language of the Composer." **Etude**, February, 1941.

SCHMIDT, HENRY L. **Scales, Harmony, and Tonality in Béla Bartók's Mikrokosmos**. Master's thesis, Eastman School of Music, 1965.

SCHIERI, F. "Béla Bartók's **Mikrokosmos**, ein Kernstück der Neuen Musiker-ziehung." **Zeitschrift für Musik** (Regensburg), February, 1954.

SIELSKA, MARYA. **Bartók's Mikrokosmos: An Analysis of its Technical Difficulties**. Master's thesis, Eastman School of Music, 1947.

STEVENS, HALSEY. **The Life and Music of Béla Bartók**. New York: Oxford University Press, revised edition, 1964.

SUCHOFF, BENJAMIN. "Bartók, Ethnomusicology and the Computer." Institute for Computer Research in the Humanities **Newsletter** (New York University), Vol. IV, No. 4, 1968.

————————————"**Bartók. Rumänische Volkslieder aus dem Komitat Bihar.** Heraus. D. Dille. Editio Musica, Budapest, 1967." **Notes** (Music Library Association, Washington, D.C.), Vol. 25, No. 3, 1969.

———————————— "Bartók's Contributions to Music Education." **Music Teaching Methods and Techniques** (Catholic University Press, Washington, D.C.), 1961; **Journal of Research in Music Education**, Vol. IX, No. 1, 1961; **Tempo** (London), No. 60, 1962.

———————————— "Bartók's Second String Quartet: Stylistic Landmark." **Nutida Musika** (Stockholm), Nos. 5-6, 1965; **American Music Teacher**, Vol. 15, No. 2, 1965.

———————————— **Béla Bartók and a Guide to the Mikrokosmos**, Vols. I-II, Doctor's thesis, New York University, 1956; Ann Arbor: University Micro-films, No. 17, 678, 1957 (see also **Dissertation Abstracts**, Vol. XVII, No. 4, 1957).

———————————— "The Computer and Bartók Research in America." **Magyar Zenetörténeti Tanulmányok** (edited by Ferenc Bónis), Vol. III. Budapest: Editio Musica, 1971; **Journal of Research in Music Education,** Vol. XIX, No. 1, 1971.

———————————— "Computer Applications to Bartók's Serbo-Croatian Material." **Tempo** (London), No. 80, 1967.

———————————— "Computerized Folk Song Research and the Problem of Variants." **Computers and the Humanities** (New York), Vol. 2, No. 4, 1968.

(SUCHOFF, BENJAMIN). "Computer-Oriented Comparative Musicology." **The Computer and Music** (edited by Harry B. Lincoln), Cornell University Press, 1970.

———————————— "Errata in the **Mikrokosmos** Publication." **Piano Quarterly Newsletter,** No. 16, 1956; **Új Zenei Szemle,** October, 1956.

———————————— "History of Béla Bartók's **Mikrokosmos.**" **Journal of Research in Music Education,** Vol. VII, No. 2, 1959.

———————————— "Interpreting Bartók's Piano Works." **Piano Quarterly Newsletter,** No. 20, 1957.

———————————— Introduction to **Béla Bartók. Pieces and Suites for Piano Duet.** New York: Sam Fox Publishing Co., 1962.

———————————— Notes to **Bartók for Two.** New York: E. B. Marks Music Corp., 1960.

———————————— "Preface to Bartók's **Rumanian Folk Music,**" **Tribuna** (Cluj, Rumania), Vol. XIII, Nos. 30-31, 1969; **Magyar Zene** (Budapest), Vol. X, No. 2, 1969; **Ethnomusicology,** Vol. XIV, 1970.

———————————— "Some Observations on Bartók's Third Piano Concerto." **Tempo** (London), No. 65, 1963.

———————————— "Some Problems in Computer-Oriented Bartókian Ethnomusicology." **Ethnomusicology,** Vol. XIII, No. 3, 1969; **Revista de etnografie si folclor** (Bucharest), Vol. 14, No. 5, 1969; **Muzsika** (Budapest), Vol. XIII, 1970.

———————————— "Structure and Concept in Bartók's Sixth Quartet." **Tempo** (London), No. 83, 1968; **Muzica** (Bucharest), 1969.

SZABOLCSI, BENCE. "Bartók és a népzene." **Új Zenei Szemle** (Budapest), September, 1950.

———————————— **Bartók Béla, Leben und Werk.** Leipzig: Verlag Philipp Reclam June, 1961.

SZELÉNYI, ISTVÁN. "Bartók Mikrokoszmosz-a." **Énekszó** (Budapest), September-October, 1941.

SZERVÁNSKY, ENDRE. "Hogyan tanulmányozzuk Bartók műveit?" **Énekszó** (Budapest), December, 1946.

TAYLOR, VERNON H. **Contrapuntal Techniques in the Music of Béla Bartók.** Doctoral dissertation. Northwestern University, 1950.

UJFALUSSY, JÓZSEF. **Bartók Béla** (Vols. I-II). Budapest: Zeneműkiadó Vallalat, 1965.

UHDE, JÜRGEN. Bartók Mikrokosmos Spielanweisungen und Erläuterungen. Regensburg: Gustav Bosse, 1954.

—————————— "Leben und Ordnung—Béla Bartók's 'Mikrokosmos'." Zeitschrift für Musik (Regensburg), 1954.

VARRO, MARGIT. "Bartók's Mikrokosmos in Retrospect." The Piano Teacher (Evanston), Vol 3, No. 4, 1961.

VINTON, JOHN. "Toward a Chronology of the Mikrokosmos." Studia Musicologica (Budapest), Vol. VIII, Nos. 1-4, 1966.

WAAGE, SUSANNE, Béla Bartóks "Mikrokosmos" med saerligt hensyn til satstekiken. Doctor's thesis, Denmark, 1963.

WEISENGRUND-ADORNO, THEODOR. "Béla Bartók: 'Mikrokosmos'." Schweizerische Musikzeitung (Zürich), 1940.

WEISSMANN, JOHN. "Bartókiana." Tempo (London), Nos. 55-56, 1960.

—————————— "Bartók's Piano Music." A Memorial Review (Boosey and Hawkes, New York), 1950.

—————————— "La musique de piano de Bartók: l'evolution d'une écriture." La Revue Musicale (Paris), No. 224, 1955.

—————————— "On Some Problems of Bartók Research in Connection with Bartók's Biography." Studia Musicologica (Budapest), Vol. V., Nos. 1-4, 1963.

WOLFF, HANS C. "Der 'Mikrokosmos' von Béla Bartók." Musica (Cassel), March, 1951.

WYKES, ROBERT A. Structural Devices in the Music of Béla Bartók. Master's Thesis, Eastman School of Music, 1949.

ZIMMERREIMER, KURT. "Der Stil Béla Bartóks." Musica (Cassel), Vol. I.

Figures in italics refer to page numbers, figures in bold-faced type indicate specific pieces as numbered in the **Mikrokosmos**.

Abstract music, *6*, **45**, **81**
Accelerando, **103**
Accents, *15*, **21** ff.
Accidentals, **8** ff., Ex. 1 ff.
Accompanying figurations, *17;*
 right hand, **74a**, **78**, Ex. 33;
 left hand, **40** ff.; both hands, **42** ff.
Adagio, **41**
Additive rhythm, *7*, **48** ff., Ex. 19,
 20 **(66)** see also Rhythm
Aeolian mode, **2b**, *5*, **8**, **21**, **36**, **67**;
 transposed, **65**, **71**, **78**, **101**, **127**
Agitato, **142**
Alla breve, **12**
Allargando, **75**
Allegretto, **37**
Allegro, **31**
Alternation of modes, see Modes
American folk music, see Folk style
Andante, **33**
Andantino, **80**
Anhemitone pentatonic scale,
 61, see also Scales
Arm coordination, **96**
Arpeggios, *17*, see also Chords
 (broken)
Assai, **58**
A tempo, **79**
Atonalists, *3*
Augmentation, **46**, **87**, **121**, **136**

Bach, J. S.: *Well -Tempered
 Keyboard*, *5;* First Partita
 (*Sarabande*), *15;* dissonance in
 his music, *17;* dedication to, **79**;
 in the idiom of *6*, **91**
Backhaus, Wilhelm, *2*
Bagpipe: Scotch and Yugoslav, **40**;
 theme in Beethoven's Sixth
 Symphony **40**; discussed, **138**;
 Bulgarian, **146**
Bartók Archives, *5*
Bartók, Béla: principles of piano
 teaching, *13;* ideas concerning
 piano playing and musicianship,
 14-15; piano works, *2-3*, *5*, **131**
Bartók, Ditta (Mrs. Béla), *18-19*
Bartók, Peter, *6*, **36**, **66**

Beethoven, L. van, *1-2*, *5*, **40**
Ben ritmato, **78**
Bimodality, see Polytonality
Bitonality, see Polytonality
Borowsky, Alexander, *2*
Bourrée, **117**
Broken chord playing, *17*, **32** ff.,
 see also Chord
Bulgarian folk music, see Folk
 songs, Folk style
Bulgarian rhythm, see Rhythm
Buzzing effects, **63**, **142**, **153**

Ca., **95**
Cadence: Yugoslav, *9*, **26**, **33**, **40**;
 plagal, **73**, **76**; unusual types of,
 87, **101**, **121**; Phrygian, **128**; see
 also Half-cadence, Dominant
 ending
Calando, **70**
Calmo, **34**
Cancrizans, **86**
Canon: **26** (explained), **28**, **30-1**, **36**,
 57, **60**, **123**, **128-9**, **136**, **150**, **153**;
 free, **35-6**, **51**, **91**
Cantabile, *16*, **69**, **87**
Change of time, *7*, see Meter
Chenée, Ann, *16*
Chopin, Frédéric, **97**
Chorale, **35**
Chord: playing, *9*, *17*; dissonant
 type of, **107**; minor seventh as a
 consonant type of, **56**, **78**; major
 and minor seventh, Ex. 30a, **31**;
 broken seventh, **97**; ninth, **134**;
 eleventh and thirteenth, **122**;
 quartal, **84**, **85**, **125** (broken), **131**,
 134-5, **144** (juxtaposed fourths),
 146; quintal, **84**, **85**, **144**,
 (juxtaposed fifths); cluster, **107**,
 130, **132-3**, **140-2**, **144**; see also
 Imitation, Mystic chord, Triads
Chromatic idiom, **91-2**, **145**
Chromaticism, **54**, **88**, **91**, **123**, **132**
Chromatic compression, **64**, **112**
Columbia University, *4–5*
Come sopra, **110**

Comma, **58**; *see also* Separating signs

Comodo, **39**

Compound mode, *see* Modes

Con: brio, **47**; *moto*, **63**; *spirito*, **69**; *gioia*, **142**

Con 8, **145**

Contrapuntal devices, *9*

Counterpoint, *16* (defined), **22** ff.

Couperin, François, *5*, *6*, **117**

Cowell, Henry, **102**

Crossed hands, **57, 87, 92, 99, 102-3, 107, 113, 117, 119-120, 126, 133, 135-6, 139, 141-2, 145-7, 151-2**

Cross-rhythm, *see* Polyrhythm

Damper pedal, *see* Pedal

Dance pieces, **31, 33, 50, 68, 72, 117, 119, 128, 130, 138-9, 148-53**

Diminuendo, **34**

Diminution, *7*, **20, 28, 46, 89, 114**

Division of the beat (*see especially*): into two parts, **12, 32, 37**, Ex. **29**; into three parts, **33, 41, 55, 107, 129, 147-8**; into four parts, **53, 77**; into five parts, **130, 138**; into six parts, **138, 147**; into seven parts, **138**; into eight parts, **140, 144**

Dohnanyi, Ernst von, *1*

Dolce, *14*, *16*, **51, 87**

Dominant ending, **37, 42, 51, 59, 73, 78, 105, 111, 113, 126**

Doppio, **140, 144**

Dorian mode, *14*, **18, 23, 31-2**; transposed, **87, 149**

Dotted *tenuto*, *14*, *16*, **87, 116-117, 127, 129, 146, 148-9**

Double flat, **88**

Double notes, *see* Passage-work

Double sharp, **102**

Duo-tonality, *see* Polytonality

Dynamic contrasts: *16*, (explained); *marcato*, **31** ff.; *marcatissimo*, **47** ff.; *sforzato*, **34** ff.; other, **148**

Dynamics: *15*, *18*; control of, **46**

Ear training, **127**

Embellishments: *17*; slow trills, **14, 63, 66-7, 71, 78-9, 83, 88, 92, 110, 134-5, 138, 142, 144, 147, 149, 151-2**; slow tremolos, **40, 133, 138, 153**; turns, **127, 130, 136, 138, 142, 148**, grace notes, **128, 134, 148, 151**

Ensemble playing: *17*; vocal or instrumental accompaniment, **14, 65, 74b, 95b, 127**; two-piano pieces, **43-4, 55, 68, 145**; two-piano transcriptions, *see* SEVEN PIECES FROM "MIKRO-KOSMOS"; pieces suitable for two-piano transcription by pupils, **45, 51, 56**

Espressione, **100**

Espressivo (touch) *14*, *16*, **51, 58**

Expressive ability of music, **14, 94**

Fermata, *15*, **37**

Finger: independence, *17* (*see also* Part-playing); control, **48, 63**; strengthening, **122**

Fingering problems, *17*; **10** ff. (especially **45, 47, 54, 127, 138, 147, 153**)

Folk Music: *3-4*, *7*

Folk songs: Balkan, **100**; Bulgarian, **115**; Hungarian, **74, 83, 112-3, 127**; Rumanian and Slovakian, *9*

Folk style: American, **151**; Arabic, **58, 62**; Hungarian, *15*, **34, 43, 65, 68, 111, 116, 128**; Oriental, **58, 62**; Rumanian, **126**; Russian, **90**; Transylvanian, **53**; Yugoslav, **40**

Form: *9-10*; free, **102, 108, 114, 118, 124, 126, 133-5, 142-5, 151**; rondo, **107, 150, 152**; rondo-variation, **57, 128, 136, 141**; theme and variations, **45, 72, 82, 87, 94-5, 128, 140, 148**

Forte, **22** ff.

Fortissimo, **47** ff.

Fortississimo, **145**

Gershwin, George, *6*, **151**

Gieseking, Walter, *2*

Grace notes, *see* Embellishments

Grave, **60**
Grazioso, **119**

Half-cadence (Yugoslav), **26, 33, 40, 58**
Hand independence, *16-17* (explained)
Hand position: *17;* change of, **8** ff.; one, **1** ff. (to **105**); interlocked, **99, 102-3, 110, 114, 120, 132-3, 141-4, 146, 148-9, 153;** *see also* Crossed hands
Hapsburg Monarchy, *3*
Harmonics, **102**
Haydn, Franz Joseph, *5*
Hexachord (Dorian), **148**
Hungarian Academy of Science, *3*
Hungarian folk music, *see* Folk Music, Folk songs, Folk style

Imitation, **22** ff.; (and especially) **23, 25, 29, 34-5, 37, 49-53, 63, 91-2, 128;** stretto-like, **58, 89, 91, 96, 114, 121, 124, 140, 145;** chordal, **73, 122, 129**
Impressionism, **109**
Il doppio, **140**
In rilievo, **55**
Intenso, **140**
Interlocked hands, *see* Hand position
Intermezzo, **111**
Intervals: playing of, *17*, **55** ff., Ex. **13** ff.; consecutive fifths, **55;** inversion and resolution of, **90;** diminished fifths, **101**
Invention, **91-2, 145**
Inversion: of parts, **23, 25, 47, 50-1, 57-8, 74, 78, 80-1, 94, 100;** melodic (reflected), **29, 38, 55-7, 64, 71, 78-80, 91, 96, 109, 114, 121-123, 129, 136, 140-4, 151,** Ex. **29c,** (*note:* **145b** is an inversion of **145a**)

Jaques-Dalcroze, *12*

Key signatures: devised (artificial), **8, 10, 15, 25, 38, 40-1, 44, 47, 50, 68, 76, 79, 82, 89, 93, 99;** change of, **57, 104;** polytonal type of, **70, 99, 105**
Kodály, Zoltán, *3-4*
Kossuth, Louis, *3*

Lamentoso, **142**
Largamente, **35**
La seconda volta, **40**
Legatissimo, **14,** *16*, **137**
Legato: 14-15, **32** ff.; touch-forms, *16*
Leggero, **113**
Lento, **32**
Liszt, Franz, *1*, *3-4*
Locrian mode, transposed, **63**
Lo stesso tempo, **87**
Lugubre, **140**
Lydian mode, **15, 37, 52, 55, 130;** transposed, **24, 33, 72, 82, 135, 145**

Marcatissimo, *15*, **40, 108**
Marcato, *15*, **31**
March, **147**
Marcia (*tempo di*), **55, 116**
Martellato, **149**
Mendelssohn, Felix, *5*
Meno, **47**
Mesto, **144**
Meter: simple and compound contrasted, **32-3;** non-coinciding (overlapping), **103, 110, 124-5, 129, 131, 133, 145-6;** change of, **12, 41, 55, 60, 71, 75, 77, 81-2, 87, 91, 93-4, 100, 102-5, 109, 111-4, 117, 120-1, 125-9, 132-3, 136-7, 140-5, 147**
Metronome, **48, 55, 113**
Mezza voce, **110**
Mezzo forte, **33**
Mezzo piano, **45**
Minuet, **50**
MIKROKOSMOS: *5*, chapter 2; and general educational theory, *11-12;* and trends in piano teaching, *12-13;* recordings of, *18-19*
Minor modes, types of, **59**
Mixolydian mode, **11, 22, 40, 48, 69, 83-4, 89;** transposed, **97, 107, 139**
Moderato, **30**
Modes: *3, 8;* alternation of, **45, 53, 56-7, 76, 93, 104, 116, 118, 120;** compound (mixed), **41-2, 50, 52, 77, 113, 115-6, 126, 128, 130, 138, 140, 146-7, 150;** *see also* entries on particular modes, as Dorian, etc.

Molto, 57
Mordent, inverted, 148
Mosso, 71, 124
Mozart, Wolfgang Amadeus, 5
Musicianship, categories of, *18*
Mystic chord, 131

Non-legato, *14*, 8 ff., touch-forms, *16*
Non-percussive touch-forms, *14*
Non troppo 48
North Africa, 58
Notation, *18*
Notturno, 97

Octaves, *see* Passage-work
Organ-point, *see* Pedal point
Oriental music, *see* Folk style
Ossia, 90, 131
Ostinato, *10*, 32-3, 40, 45, 47-8, 64,
    69, 80, 83, 90, 97, 113, 138, 146-8,
    150

Part-playing: in the right hand, 78,
    85, 125, 127; in the left hand, 41,
    62-3, 71, 81, 95, 106, 115, 128,
    139, 140, 147; in both hands,
    56 ff., Ex. 14, 19, 24
Passage-work: *17*; double-notes,
    67, 71, 73, 112, 129, 131, 134-5;
    octaves, 113 (*ossia*), 145, 147-8,
    151, 153; scales and arpeggios, 77,
    79, 98, 102, 114, 116-9, 121, 128,
    130, 138-140, 143-4, 148-9; triads,
    69, 73, 120, 151, 153, Ex. 21, 23
Pedal: damper, 47, 64, 83-4, 97, 102,
    107, 109, 111, 116, 119, 122, 126,
    133, 136, 143-4, 146, 153, Ex. 11,
    22; half-depressed damper (half
    pedal) 110, (137), 140; *ad. lib.*
    (damper), 138, 148-9, Ex. 33;
    sostenuto (*pedale prolungato*), 107,
    109, (147)
Pedalling (explained), *17*
Pedal point, 128, 141, 153
Pentachord, 81, 86, 92, 103, 108
Pentatonic scale, *see* Scales
Percussive touch-forms, *14*
Perpetuum mobile, 135
Phrasing, *9*, *15*, *18*, 9, 20, 24;
    see also Separating signs
Phrygian mode, 7, 28, 34, 46, 129;
    transposed, 137; *see also* Cadence

Piacevole, 80
Pianissimo, 46
Piano, 23
Piano School (*Zongora Iskola*), 5, *11*
Più, 43
Plagal ending, *see* Cadence
Pochettino, 125
Pochissimo, 119
Poco a poco, 95
Polyrhythm, *7*, 97, 130, 138, (55/I
    vs. 55/II)
Polytonality, *8*, 12, 30, 33, 42,
    51, 59-64, 66, 70-1, 73-5, 79, 81,
    86, 90, 92, 94, 99-103, 105-6,
    108-10, 114, 117, 119, 121-2,
    124-5, 131, 133, 139, 141-4, 148,
    152-3
Portamento (*portato*), *14*, *16*, 95a,
    116, 148
Pralltriller, *see* Mordent, inverted
Pre-Classic style, 89
Prestissimo, 103
Presto, 103
Prix Rubinstein (*1905*), 2
Program music, *6*, *71*, 15, 24, 47,
    51, 63, 65, 72, 84, 88, 94, 107-9,
    125, 130, 138-9, 142, 144, 147
Prokofiev, Serge, 133
Prol. Ped., 110
Pupils: not for the average, 46, 63,
    86, 133; difficult for some, 99;
    for unusual, 143; with great
    control, 144
Purcell, Henry, 5

Quasi a tempo, 129
Quartal harmony, *9*, 131

Rallentando, 95
Rep. ad libitum, 103
Reschofsky, Alexander, 5, *11*
Retrograde, 84, 86, 92, 96
Rhythm, *7*, *15*, *18;* additive and
    divisive compared, 66, (Ex. 9-10),
    103; Bulgarian, 113, 115, 148-153;
    see also Additive rhythm,
    Polyrhythm
Rinforzato, 148
Risoluto, 53
Robusto, 92
Romantic Period, 80

Royal Academy of Music
(Budapest), *1-2*, *3*, *5*
Rubato, **102**
Rumanian folk music, *see* Folk
style
Russian folk music, *see* Folk style

Sandor, György, *19*
Scales: *8;* chromatic, **54**, **64b**;
devised (artificial) **10**, **25**;
pentatonic, **61**, **66**, **78**, **105**, **127**,
131; Oriental, **59**, **(62)**; whole-
tone, **136**; *see also* Modes,
Passage-work
Scarlatti, Domenico, *5*
Scherzando, **82**
Scherzo, **82**
Schoenberg, Arnold, *4*, **102**
Schubert, Franz, *5*
Schumann, Robert, *5-6*, **80**
Scorrevole, **85**
Scriabin, Alexander, **67**, **131**
Secco quasi pizz., **124**
Sempre, **41**
Senza, **47**
Separating signs, *15*, **21**, **58**, **94**
SEVEN PIECES FROM
"MIKROKOSMOS", **69**, **113**, **123**,
127, **135**, **145-6**
Sforzato, *14*, **25**, **34**, **102**, **124**
Simile, **47**
Sin al fine, **145**
Smorzando, **91**
Sonoro, **93**
Sopra, **85**
Sostenuto, **110**
Sotto, **85**
Staccatissimo, *14*, **39**, **76**, **80**, **102**,
124, **146-7**, **150**
Staccato, *14*, **38** ff., Ex. **5** ff.
Strauss, Richard, *4*
Stravinsky, Igor, **83** (*Petrouchka*),
105 (*Le Sacre du Printemps*)
Strepitoso, **47**
Stretto, **81**, **91**, **124**, **140**, **145**

Stretto-like, *see* Imitation
Stringendo, **136**
Subito, **45**
Syncopation, *7*, *15*, **9** ff.

Technique, categories of, *16-17*
Tempo, *14-15*, *18*
Teneramente, **36**
Tenuto, *14*, *16*, **37** ff.; *see also*
Dotted *tenuto*
Tetrachord (Aeolian), **101**
Thomán, Stephen, *1*, *5*
Thumb crossing, **98**
Tonality, *8*
Tornando, **129**
Touch, *14*, *16*, **123**
Touch-forms: types of, *14*, *16;*
combined, *16*, **38** ff., Ex. **12**,
32-33
Transylvanian folk music, *see*
Folk style
Tremolos, *see* Embellishments
Triads, **69**, **73**, **102**, **116**, **120**, **127**,
133, **143**, **146**, **148-9**, **151-3**,
Ex. **21-3**, **32-3**
Trianon, Treaty of, **53**
Trills, *see* Embellishments
Tritone, *9*
Turns, *see* Embellishments
Twelve-tone music, *3*, *6*

Un poco più mosso, **71**

Vecsey, Franz von, *4*
Vivace, **44**
Vivacissimo, **140**
Vivo, **146**

Wagner, Richard, "Magic Fire"
theme from *Die Walküre*, **100**

Yugoslav folk music, *see* Cadence,
Folk style, Half-cadence

Zongora Iskola, *5*, *11*